The Best of

ERNIE HAASE & SIGNATURE SOUND

Volume 1

Songbook

Musical arrangements by Wayne Haun
Music Transcriptions and Engraving by MacMusic, Inc.
Kimberly Meiste, Editor
Cover Design: Doug Bennett

lillenas
PUBLISHING COMPANY

Contents

Get Away, Jordan

Originally from the album "Get Away, Jordan"

Words and Music
Spiritual

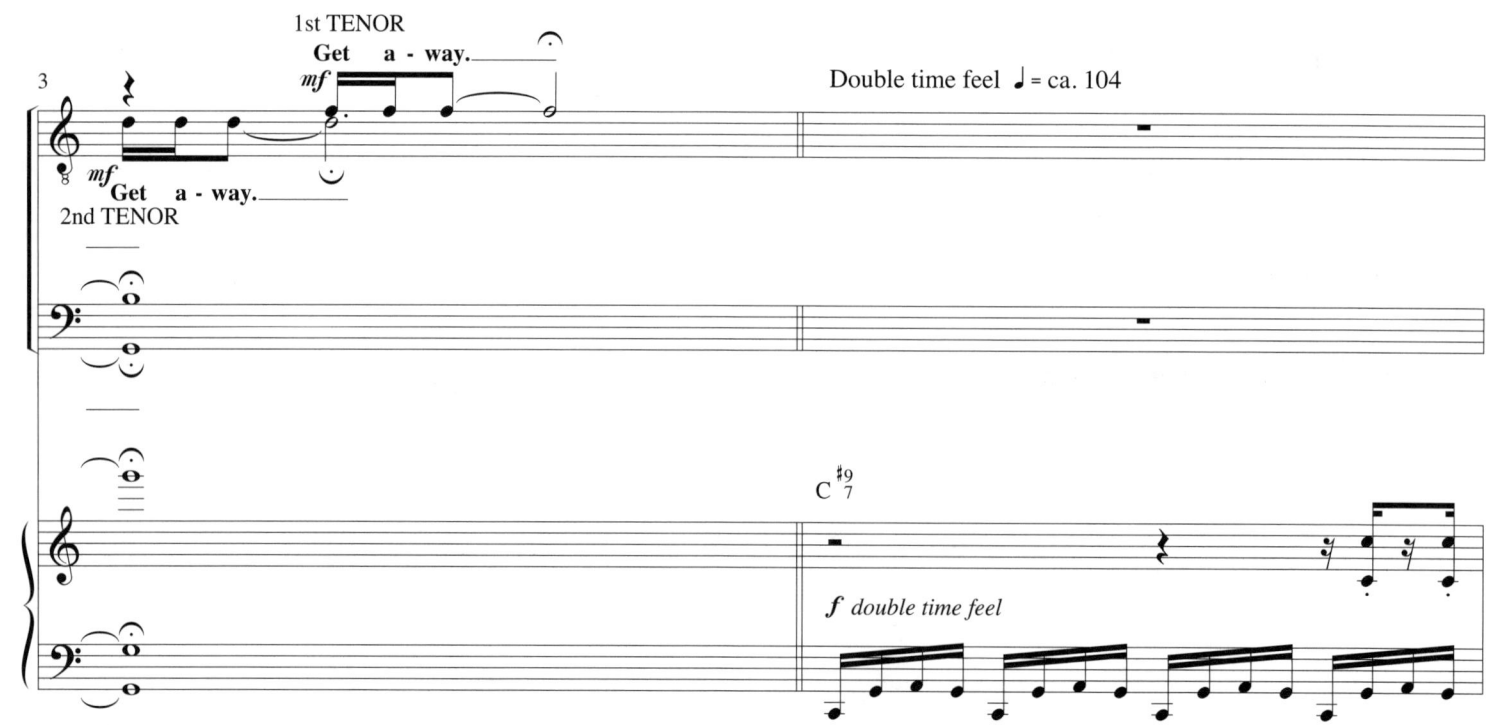

NOTE: If using more than 4 voices the first 3 measures can be stacked with each phrase.

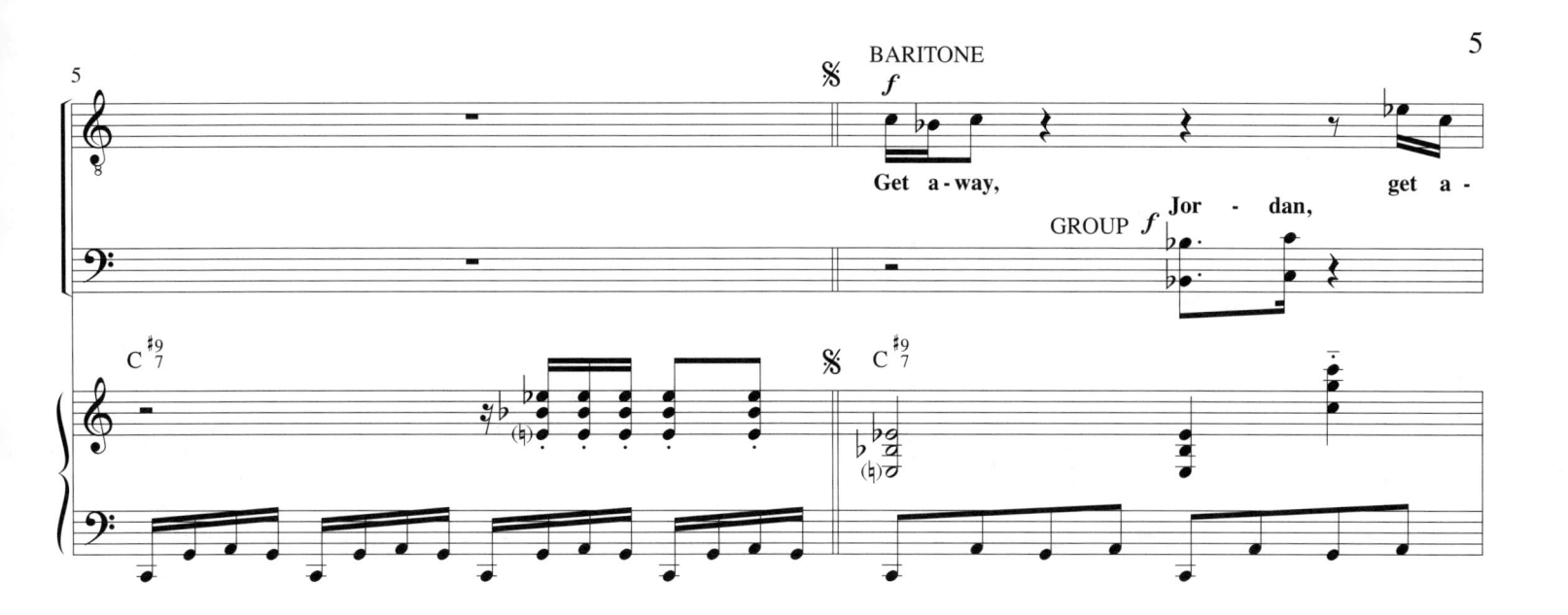

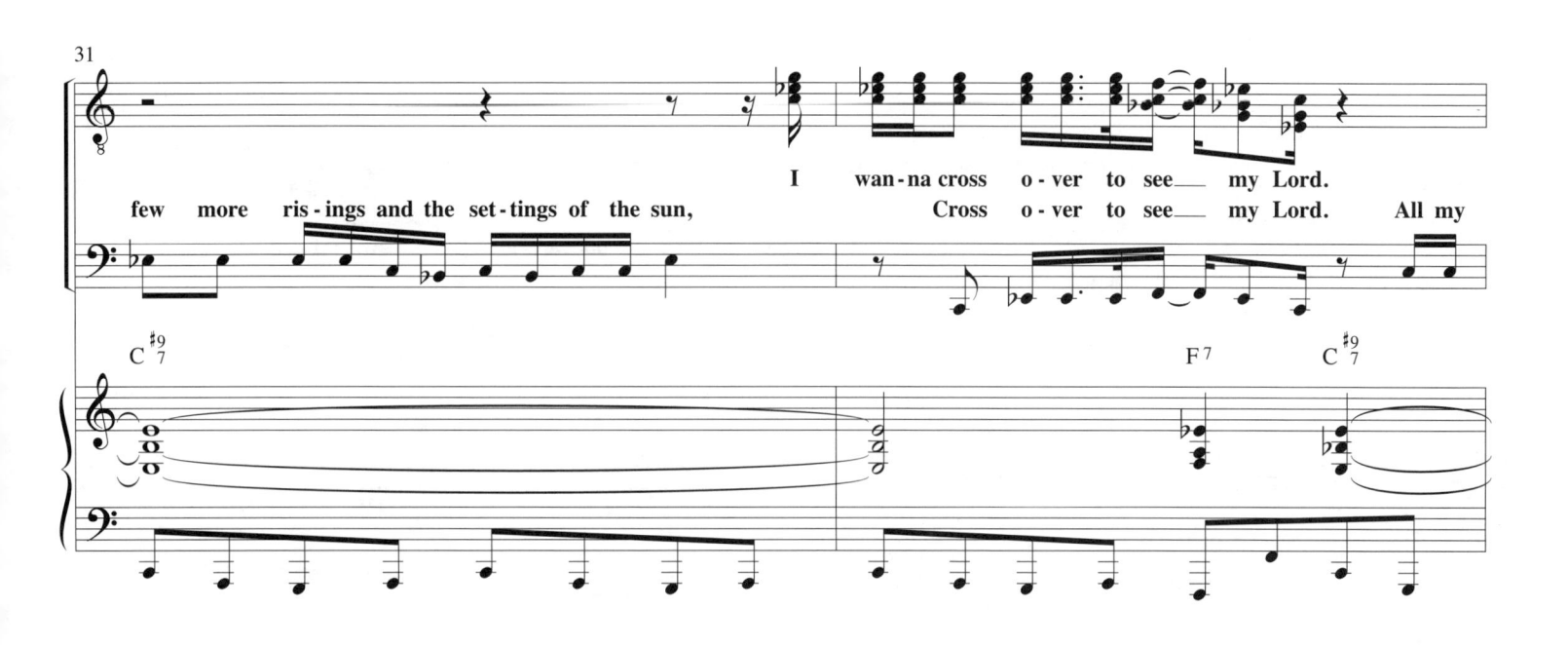

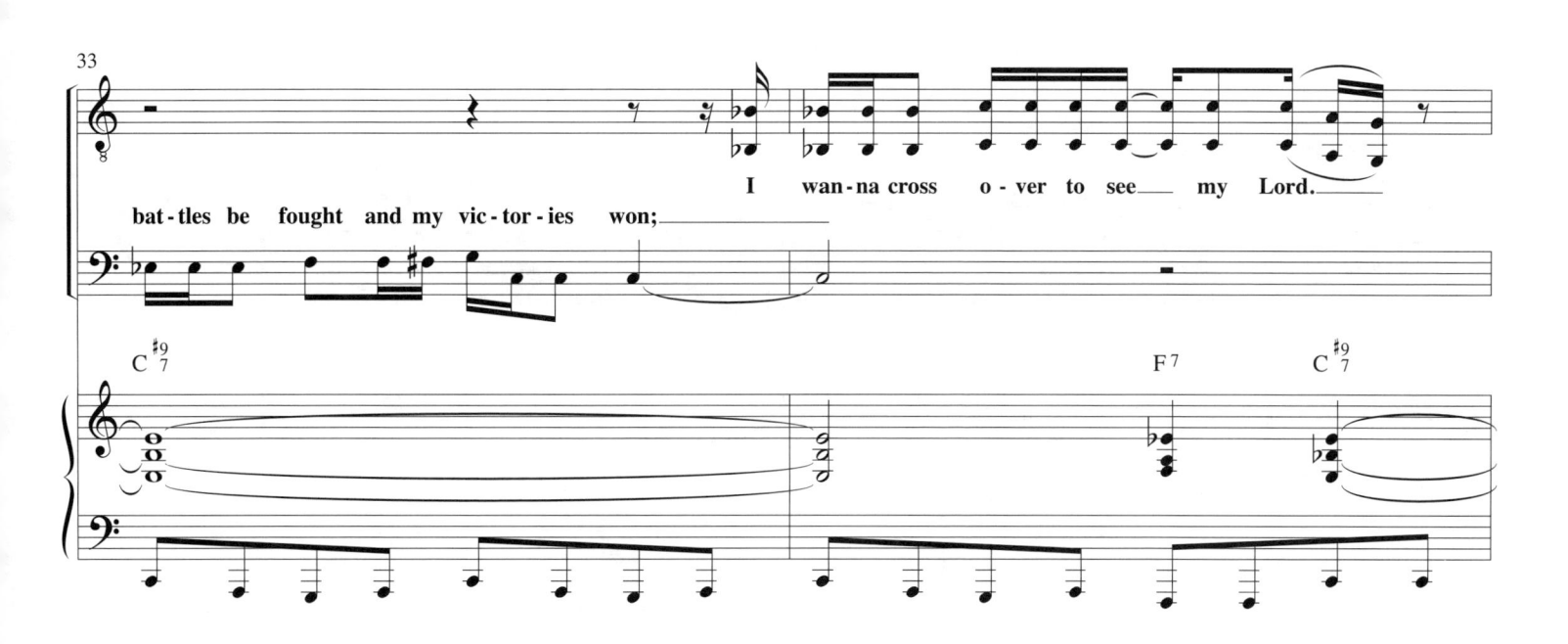

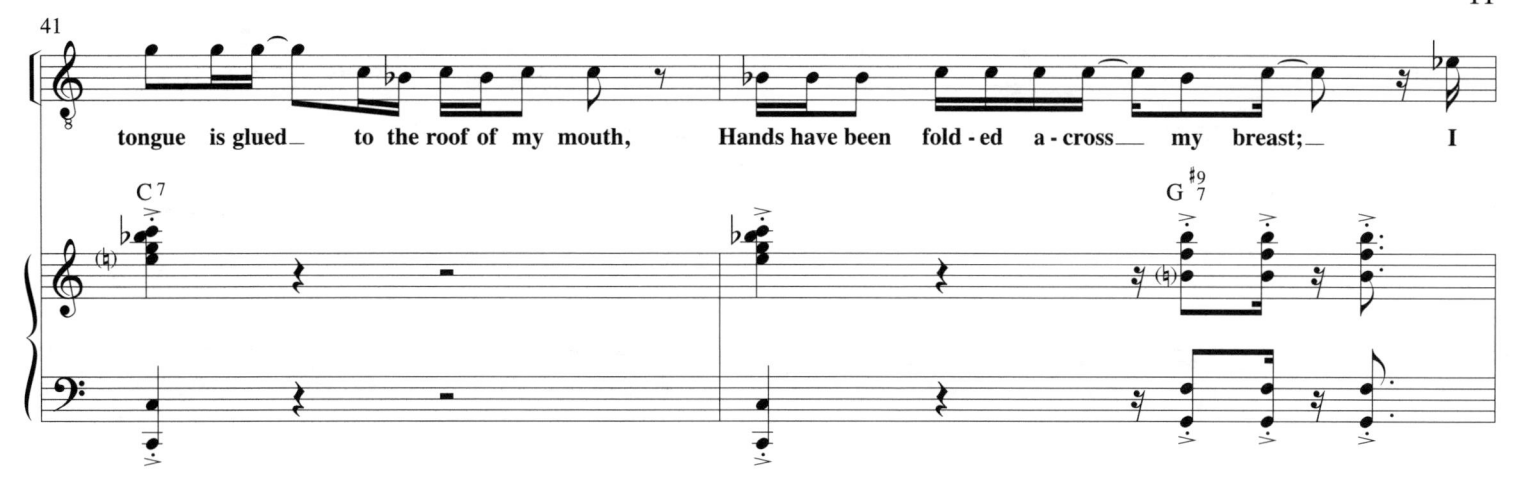

Tell me Jor - dan deep and wide, But I told mom I'd meet her on the oth - er side.___

1st TENOR

Get a - way,___ get - a, get - a, get a - way.___ Get a -

GROUP

Get a - way, Jor - dan, Get a - way, chil - ly Jor - dan,

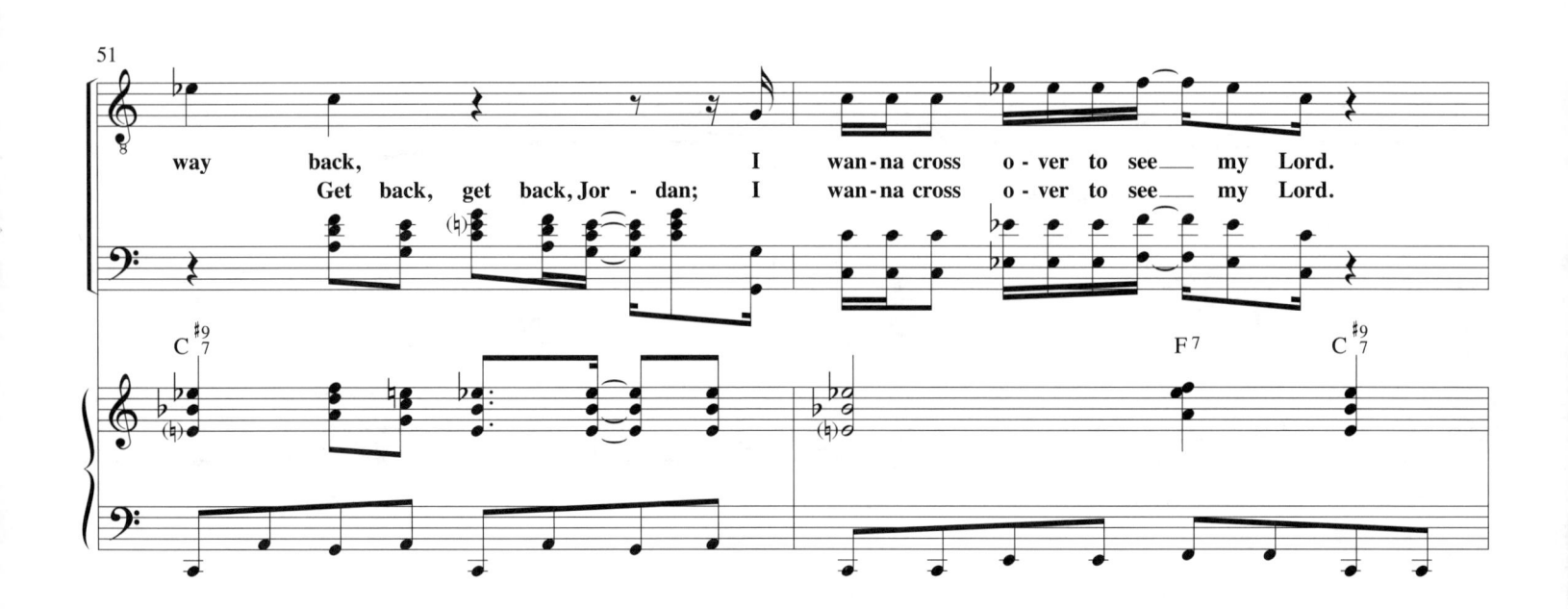

way back, I wan - na cross o - ver to see___ my Lord.

Get back, get back, Jor - dan; I wan - na cross o - ver to see___ my Lord.

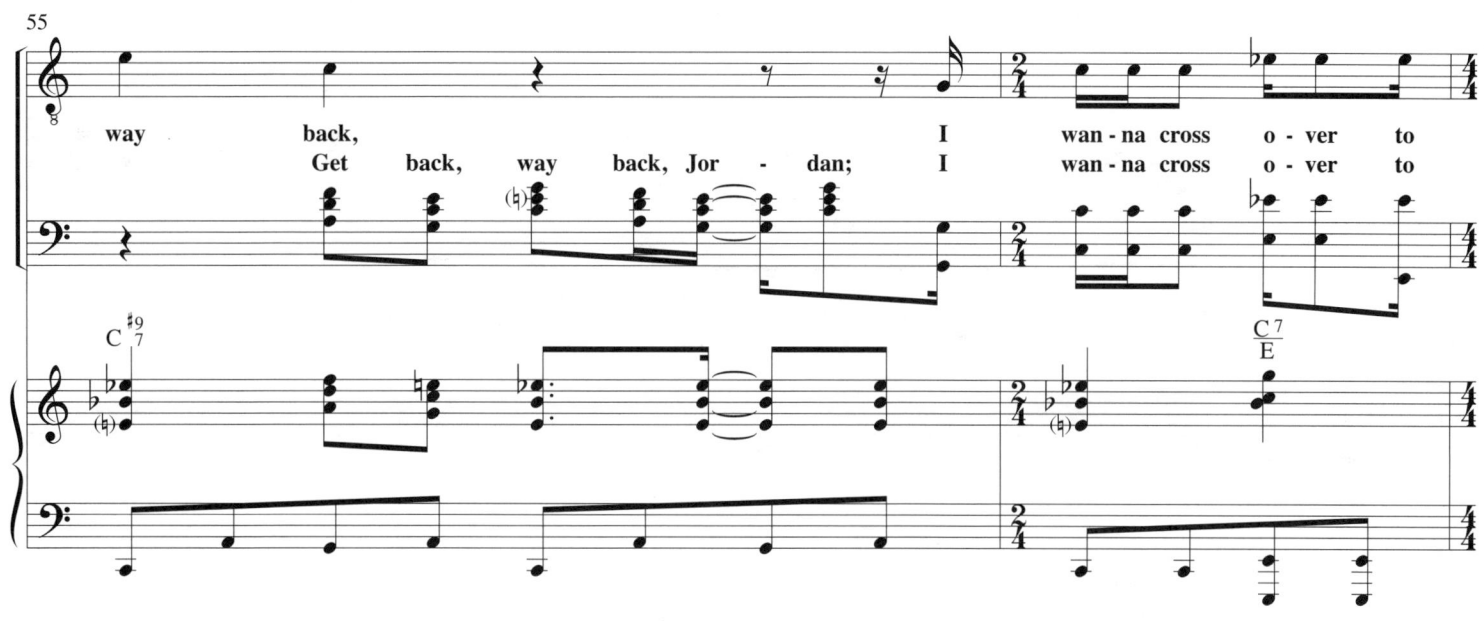

Stand by Me

Originally from the album "Get Away, Jordan"

Words and Music Unknown

Arr. © Ernie Haase/Ernie Sig Sound Music/BMI

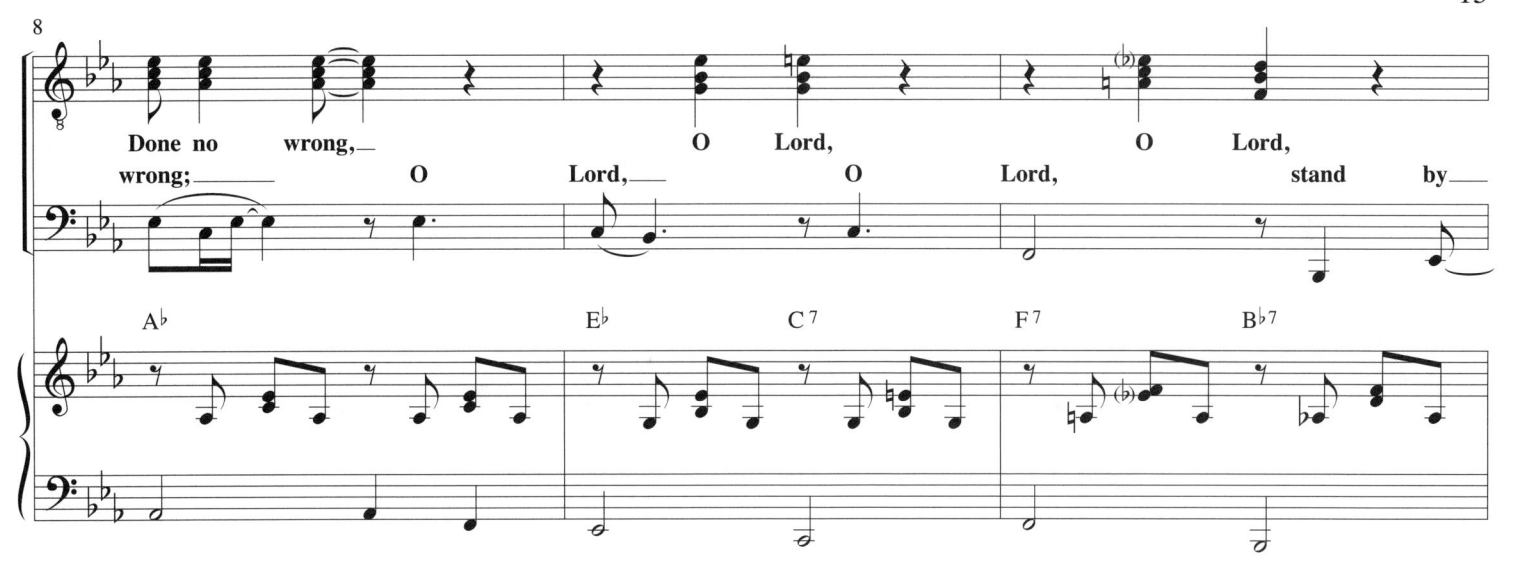

stand by me,____ help me to bear this load, this heav-y load;
yeah,____ help me to bear;_____ And if I

If I stum-ble, Lord,____ pick me up,____ Help me to drink this
stum-ble, pick me up, Help me to drink,_____

bit-ter cup; O Lord, O Lord,
yeah, 'Til I reach my home in glo - ry,____ stand by

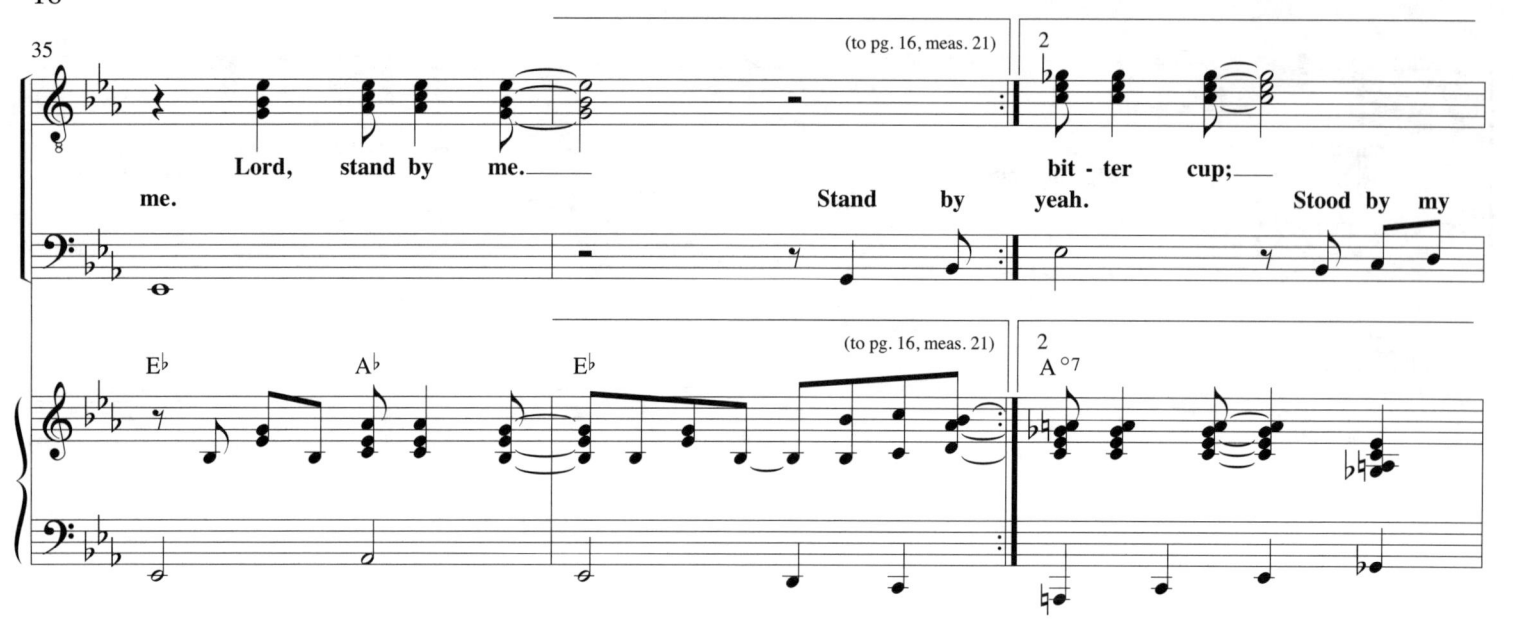

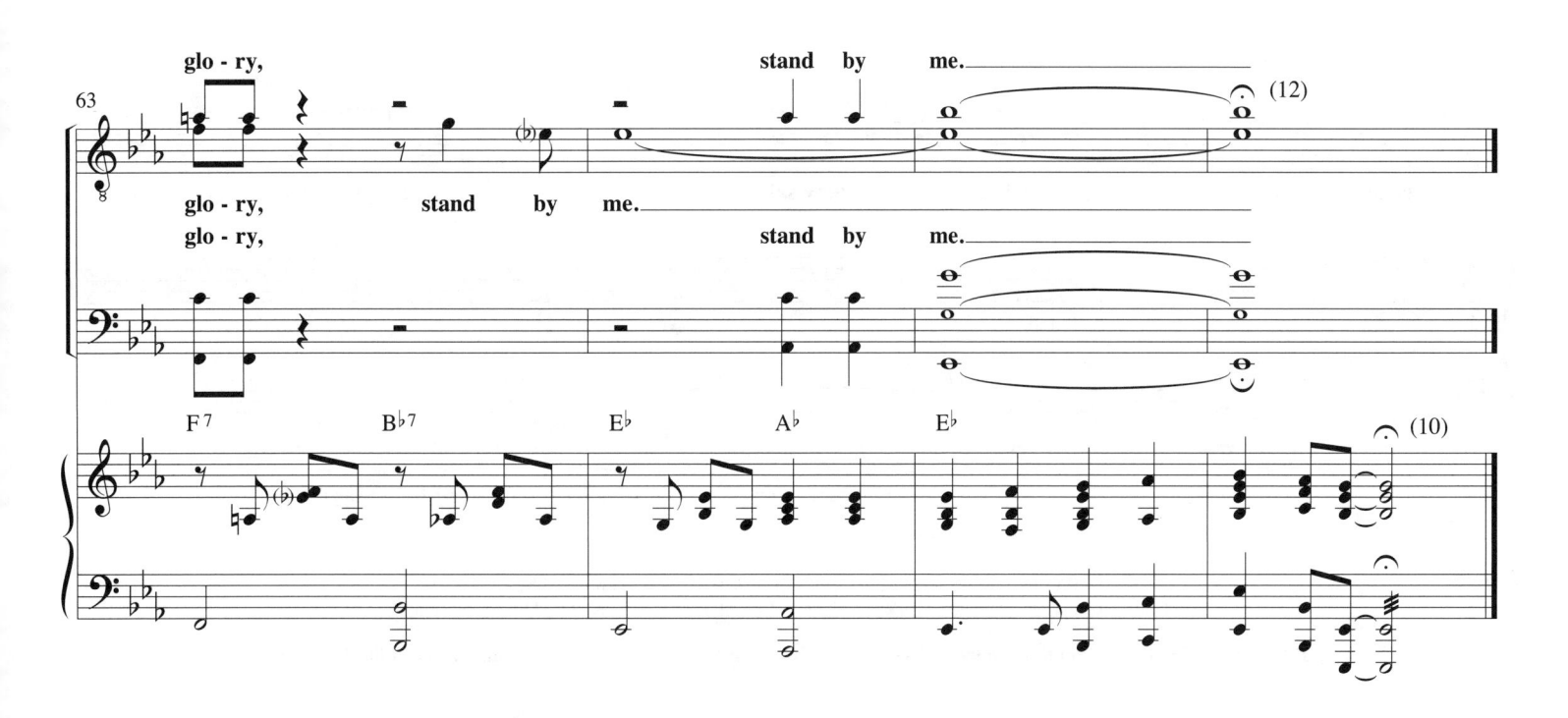

Then Came the Morning

Originally from the album "Self Titled"

Words and Music by
WILLIAM J. GAITHER, GLORIA GAITHER
and CHRIS CHRISTIAN

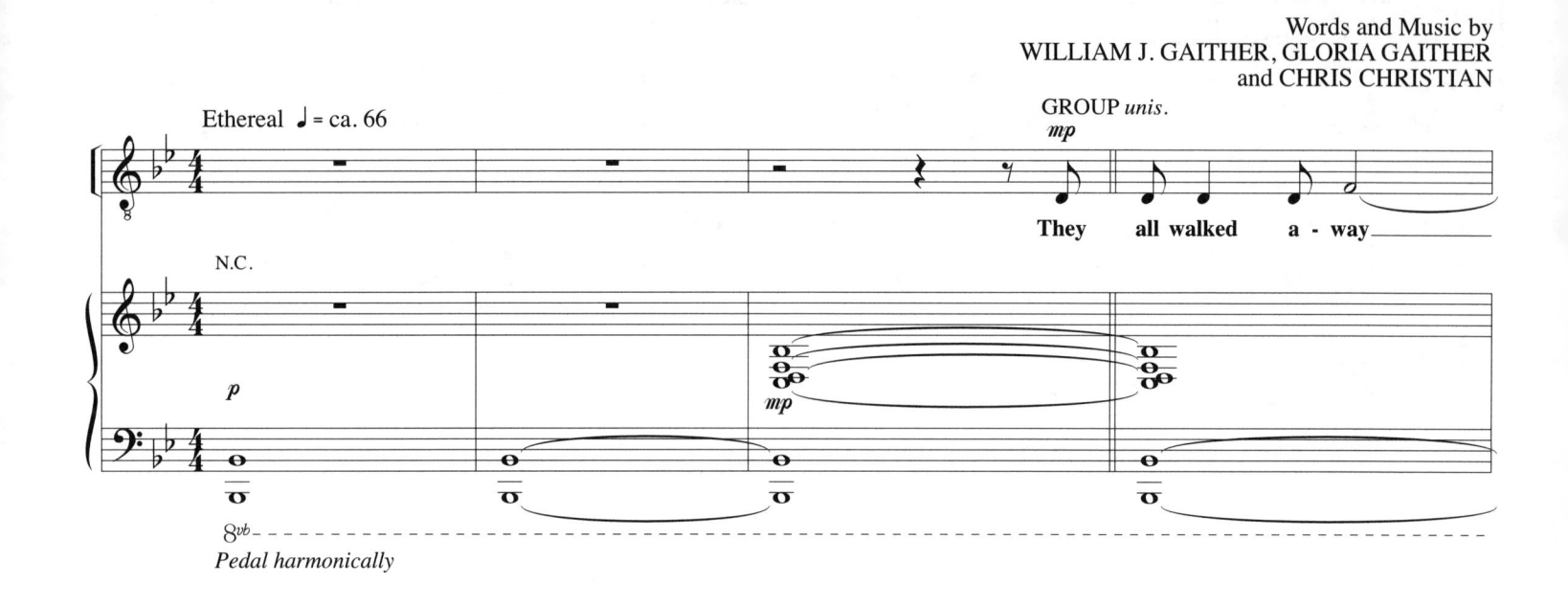

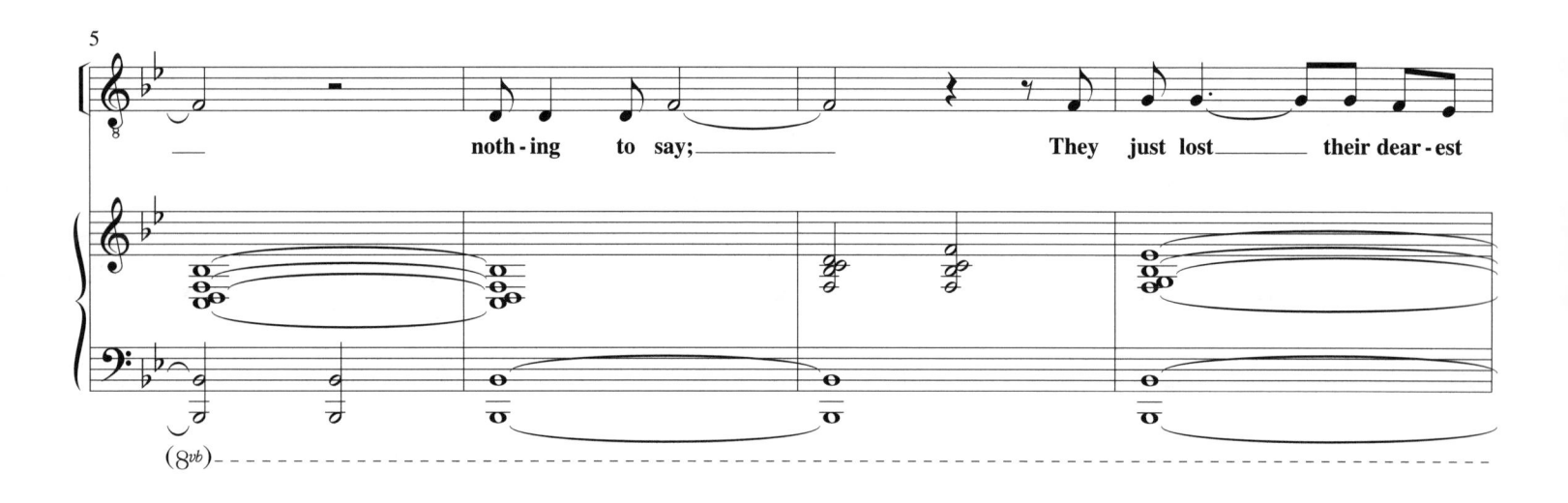

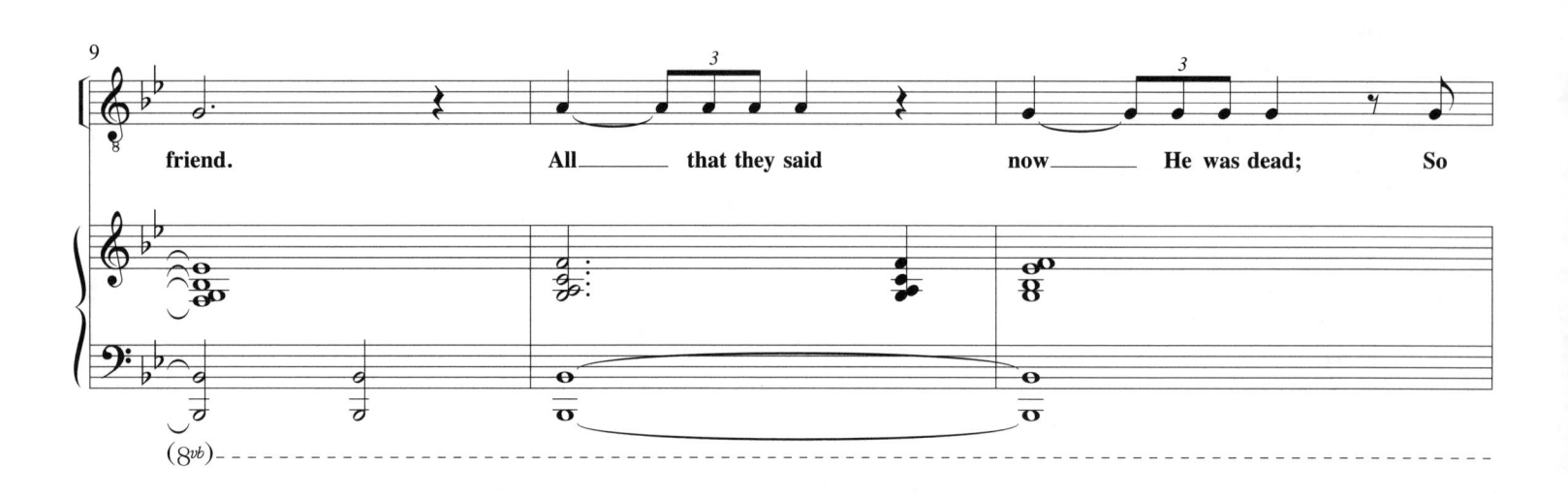

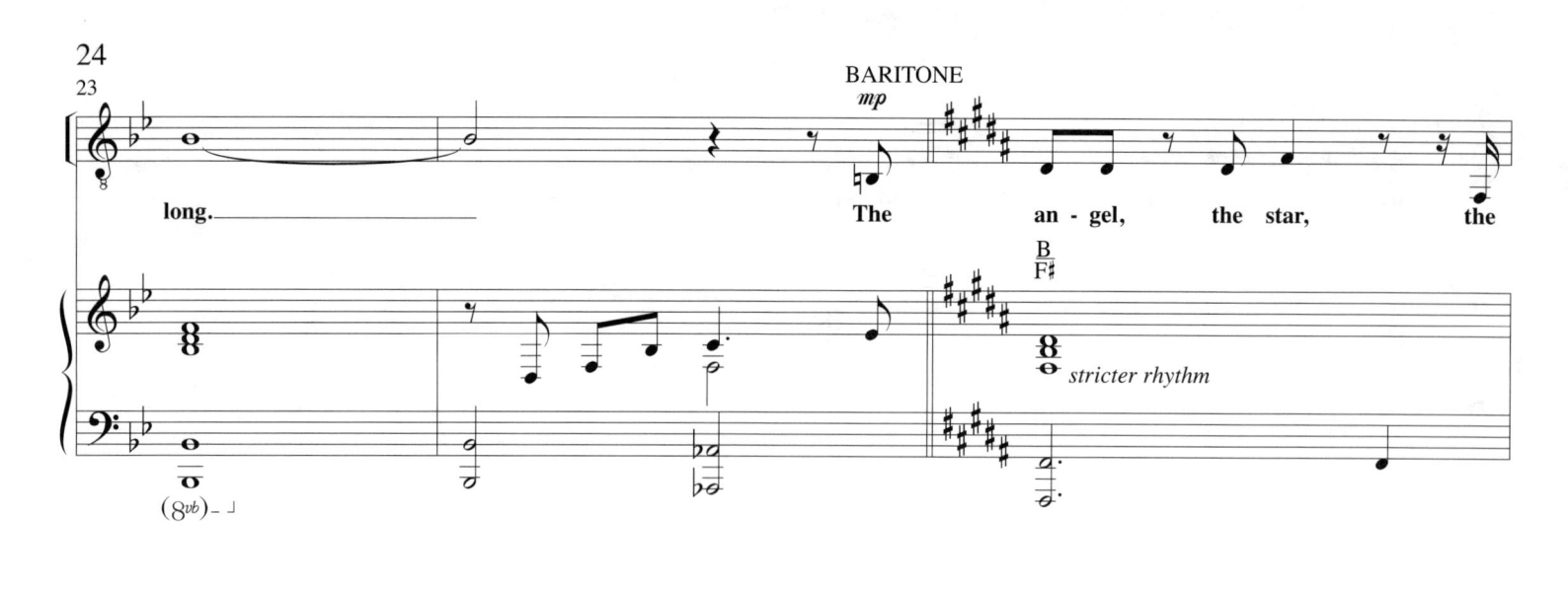

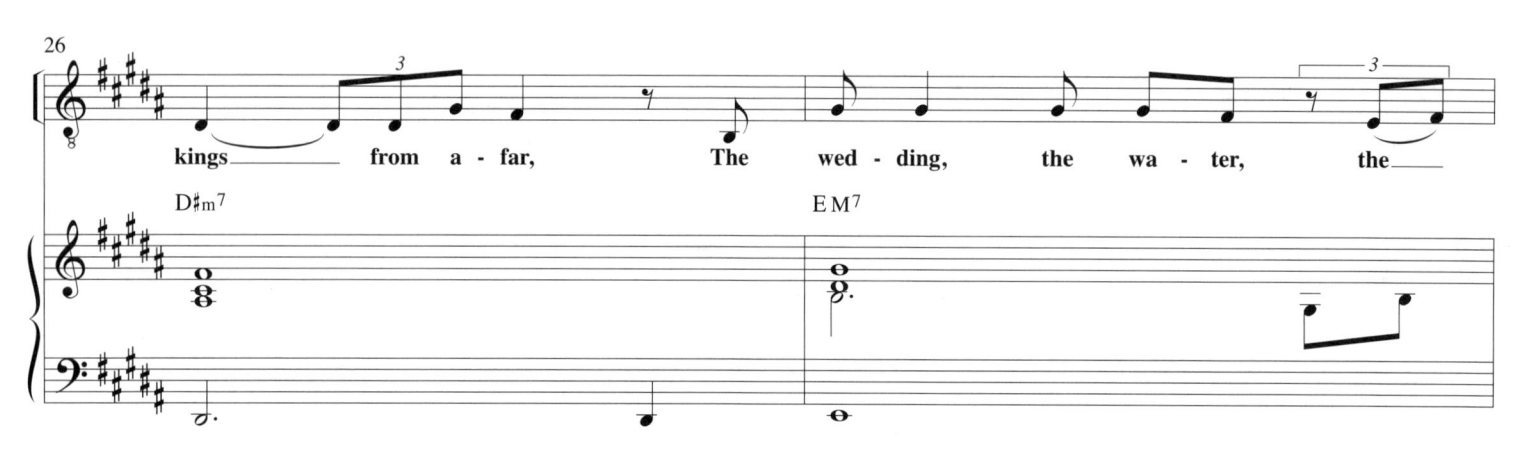

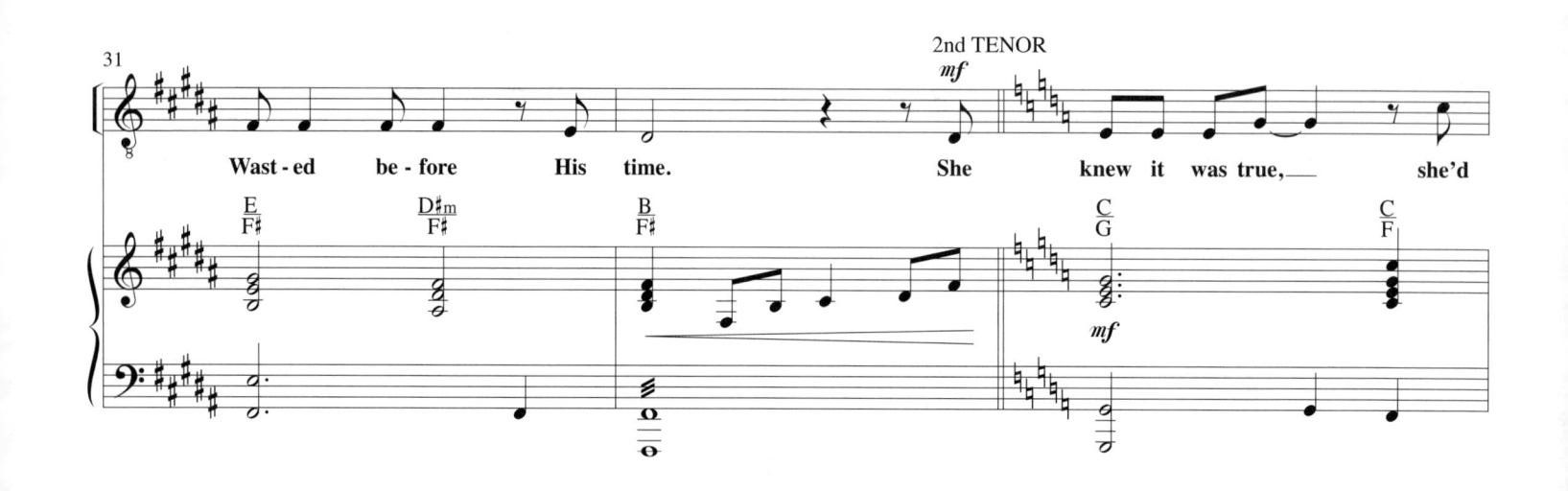

The stone was rolled a-way, hope rose with the dawn.

Then came the morn - ing, shad-ows van-ished be - fore the sun;

Death had lost and life had won for morn - ing had

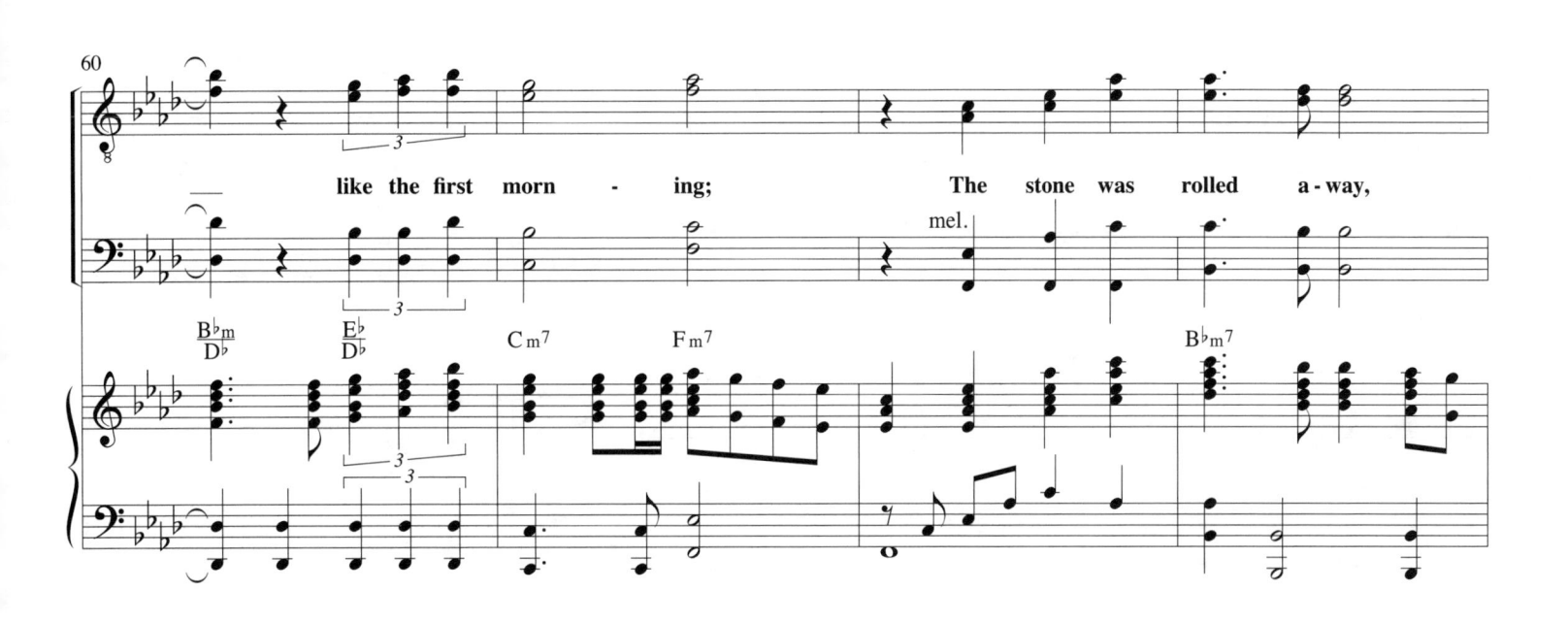

morn - ing, shad-ows van-ished be - fore the sun;

Death had lost and life had won for morn - ing had

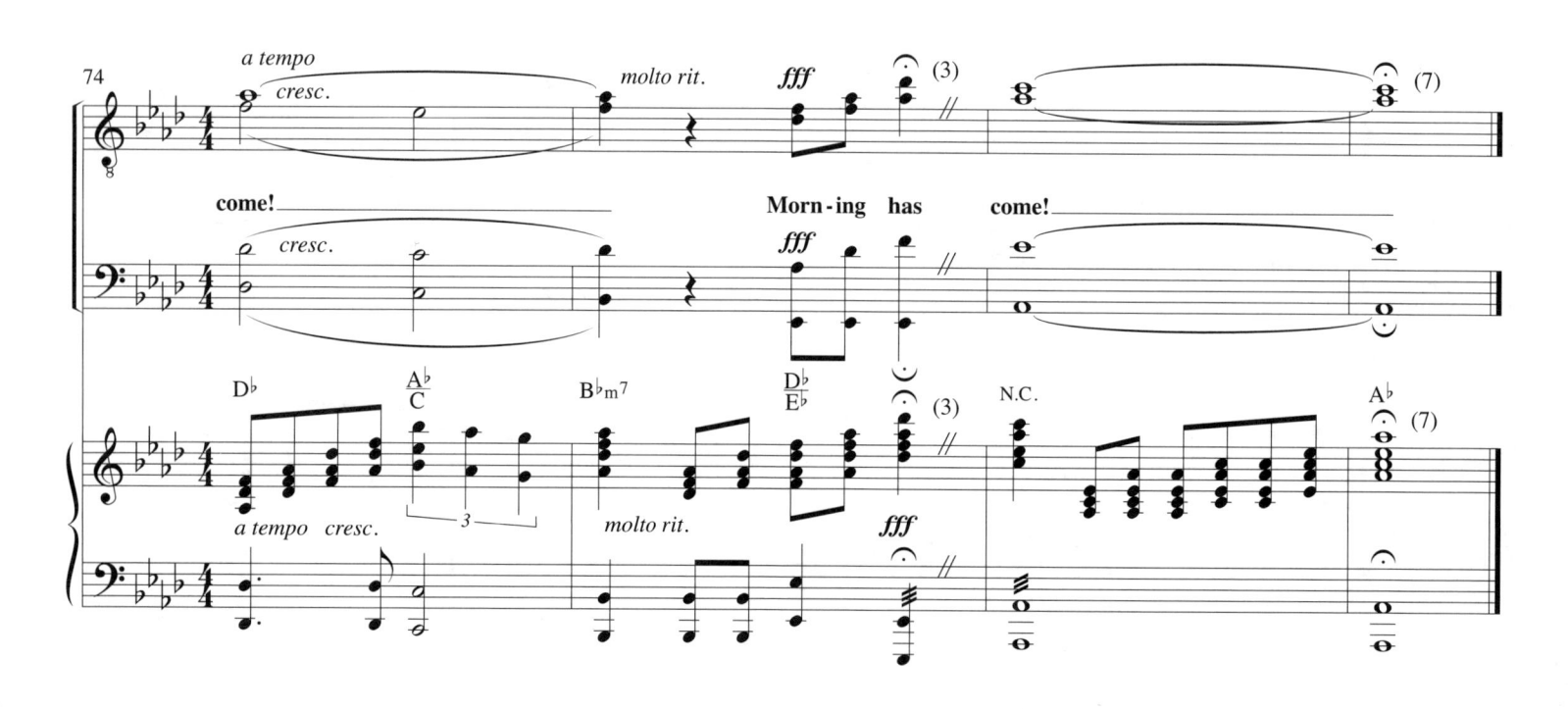

come! Morn-ing has come!

Pray for Me

Originally from the album "Self Titled"

Words and Music by
DIANNE WILKINSON

PLEASE NOTE: Copying of this product is NOT covered by CCLI licenses. For CCLI information call 1-800-234-2446.

*Optional 4th Group part in cued notes alternating between the 2nd Tenor and Baritone.

Trying to Get a Glimpse

Originally from the album "Self Titled"

JAMES WETHERINGTON
SUZANNE JENNINGS 3rd Verse

JAMES WETHERINGTON

Southern gospel feel ♩ = ca. 96

TENORS *and* BARITONE

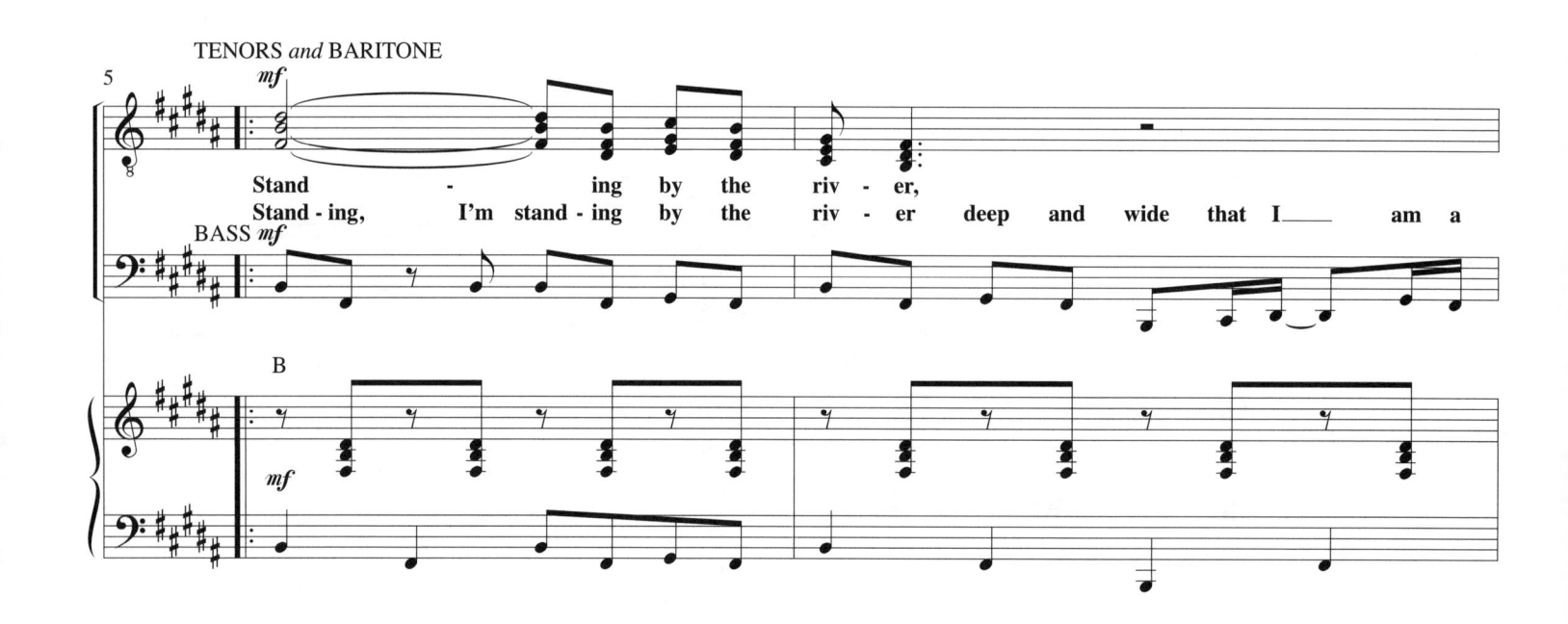

Stand - ing by the riv - er,
Stand - ing, I'm stand - ing by the riv - er deep and wide that I___ am a

(to pg. 38, meas. 5)

Look-ing for the light of my Sav - ior up in the sky.

B   G♯7   C♯7   F♯7   B N.C.

Stand-ing there wait-ing for the boat-man read-y to go, I'm read-y to go.   To heav - en,

Oo,   Of Jor - dan,

Stand-ing there wait-ing for the boat-man on a that shore, on that shore.

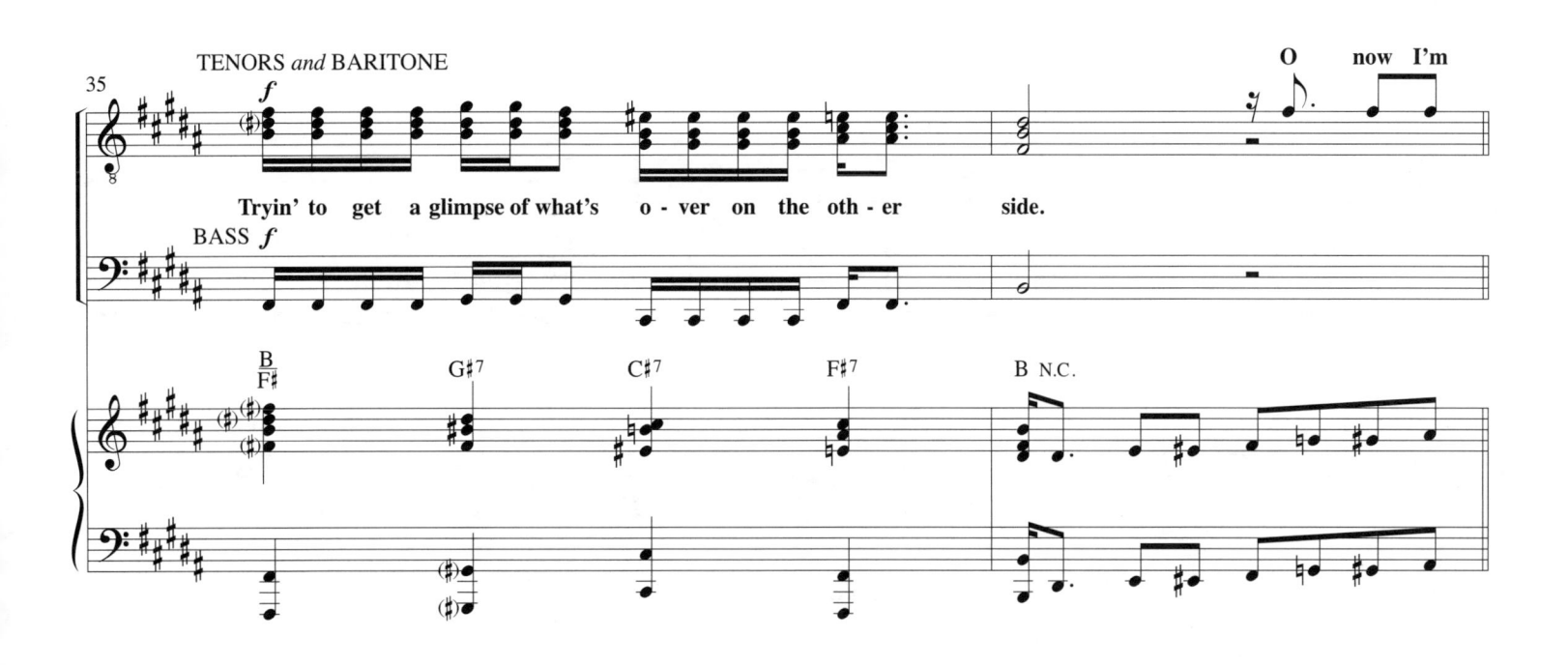

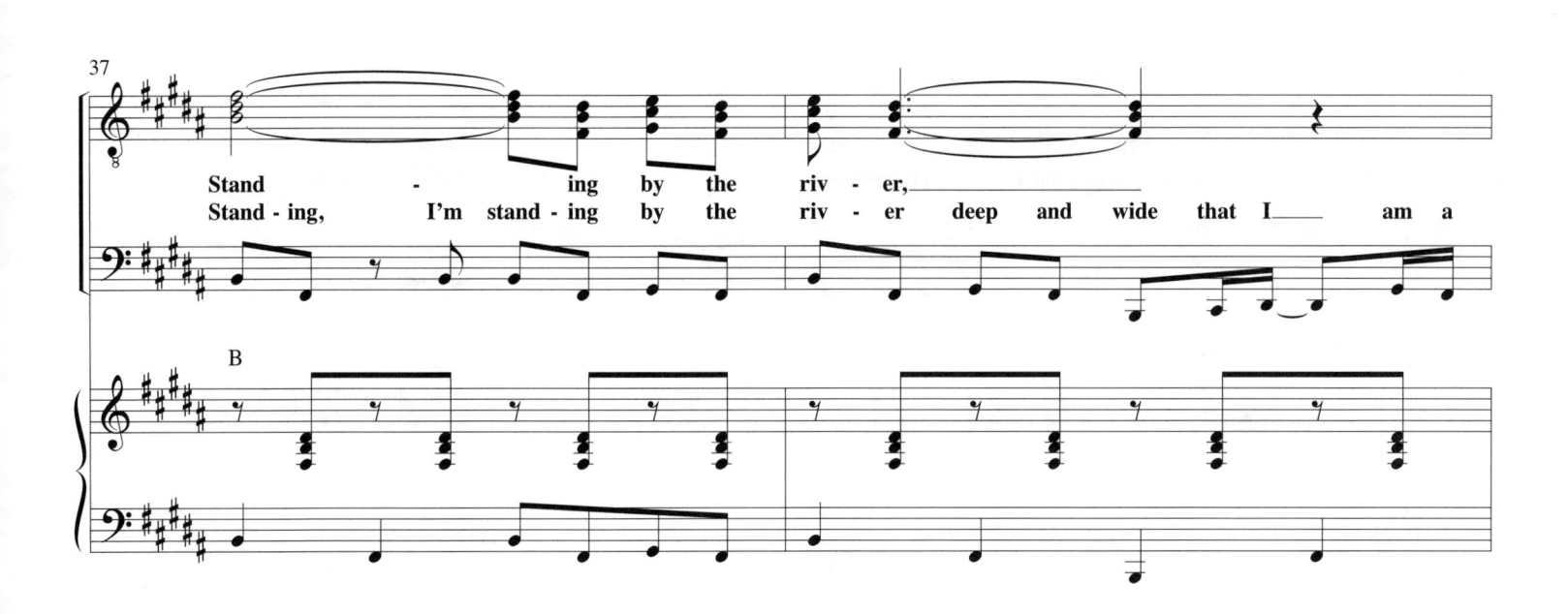

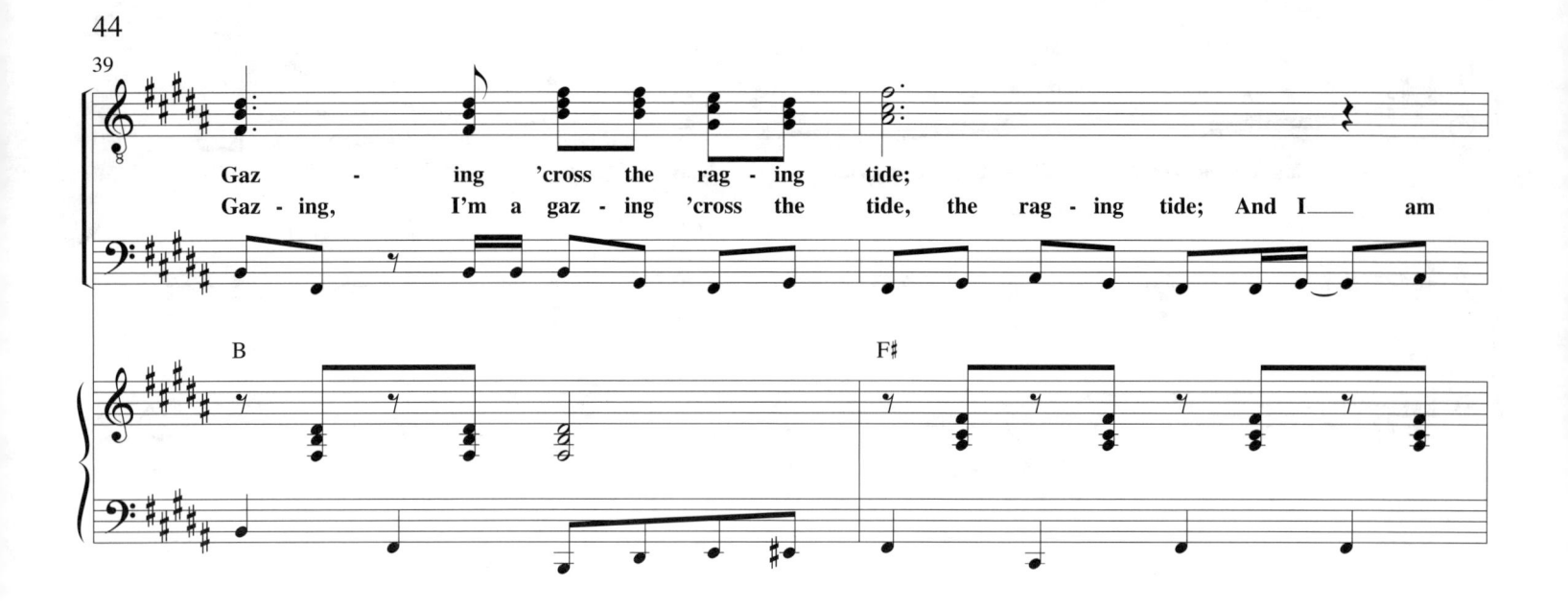

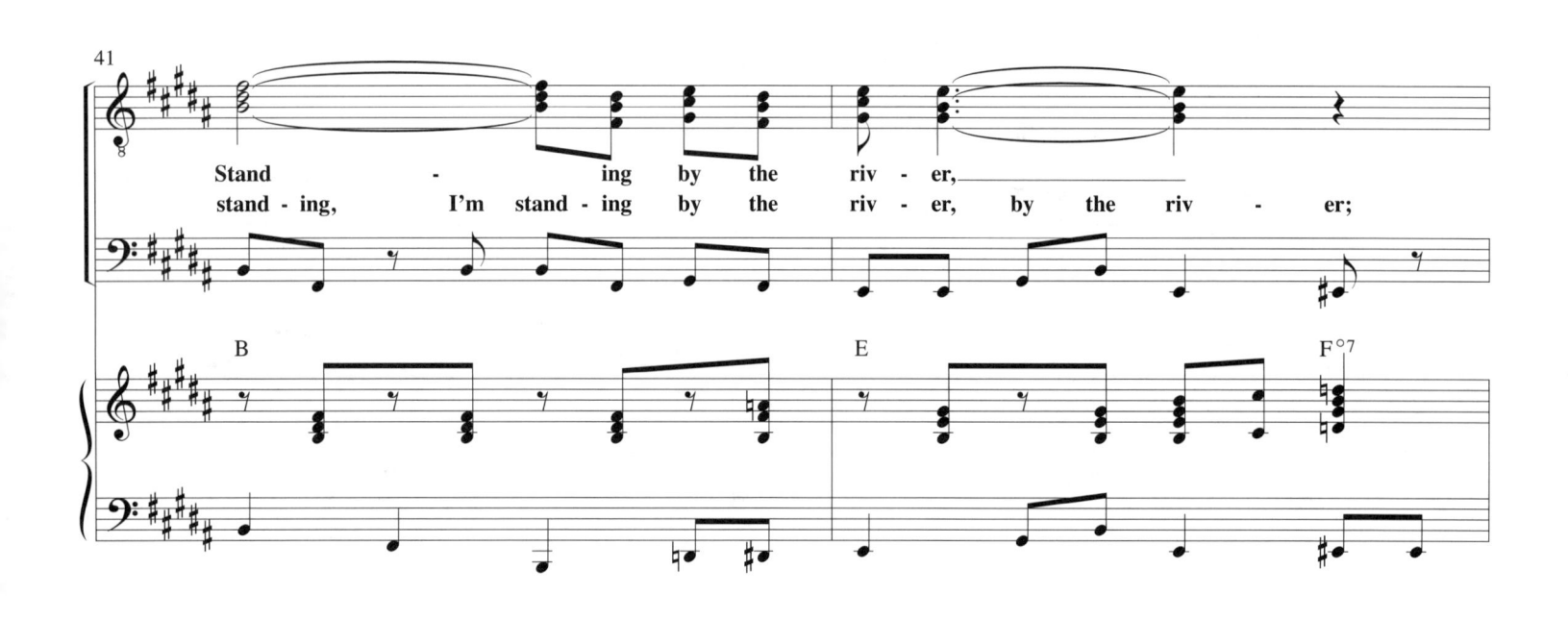

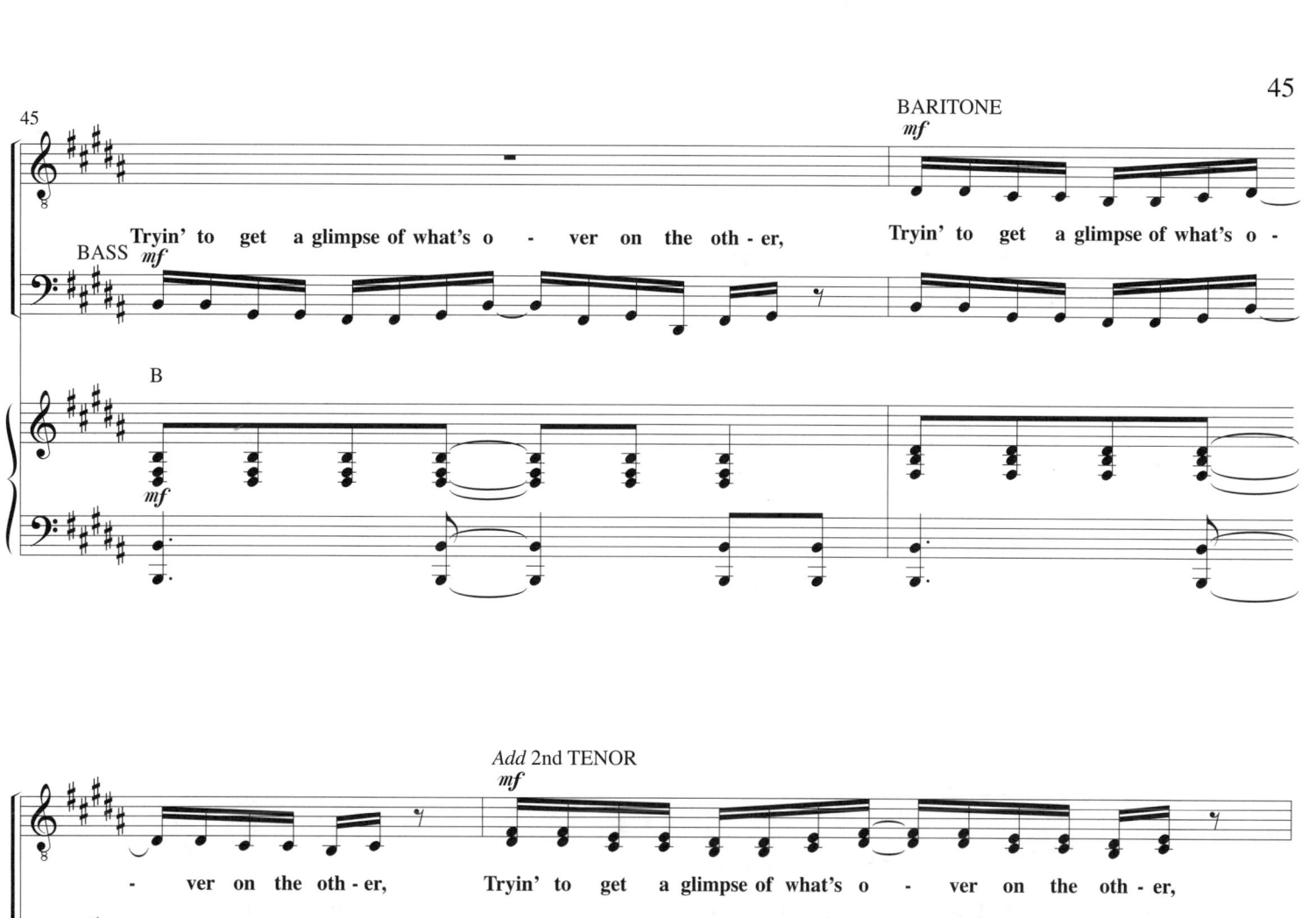

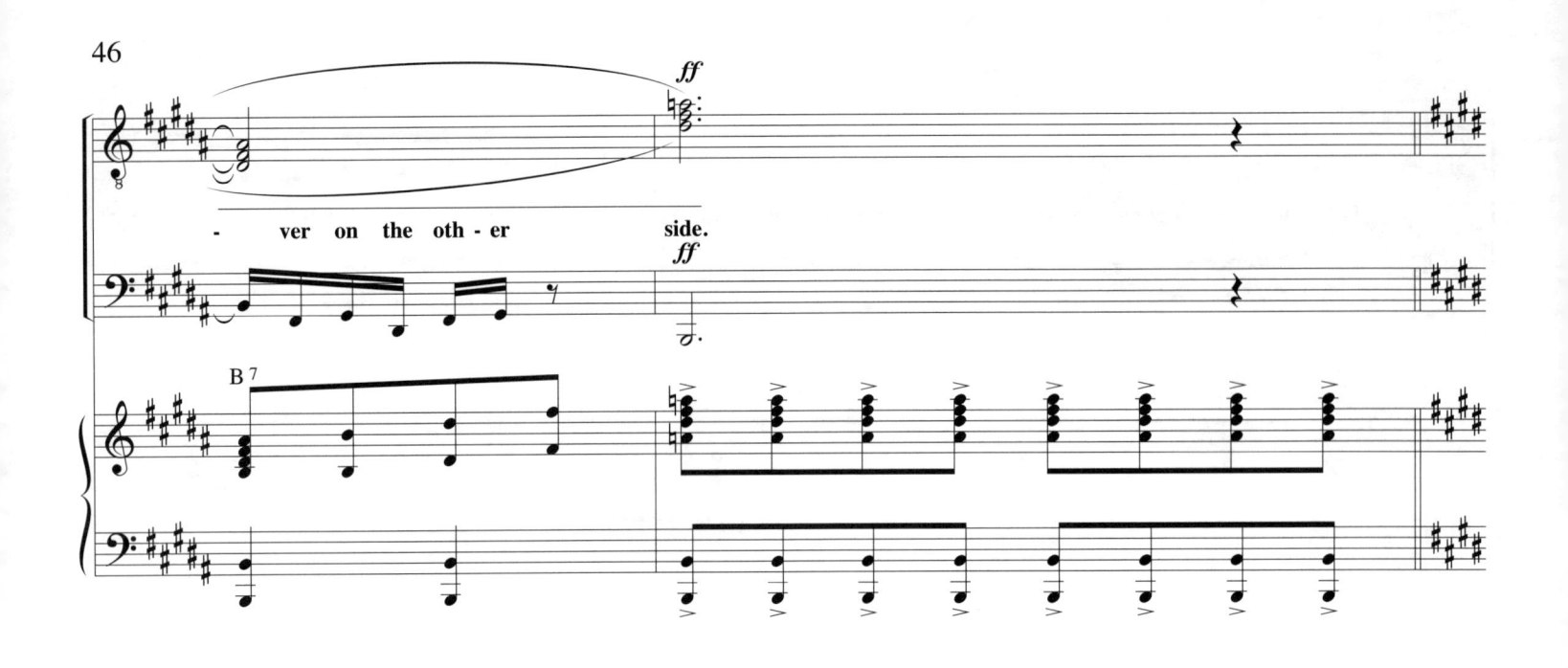

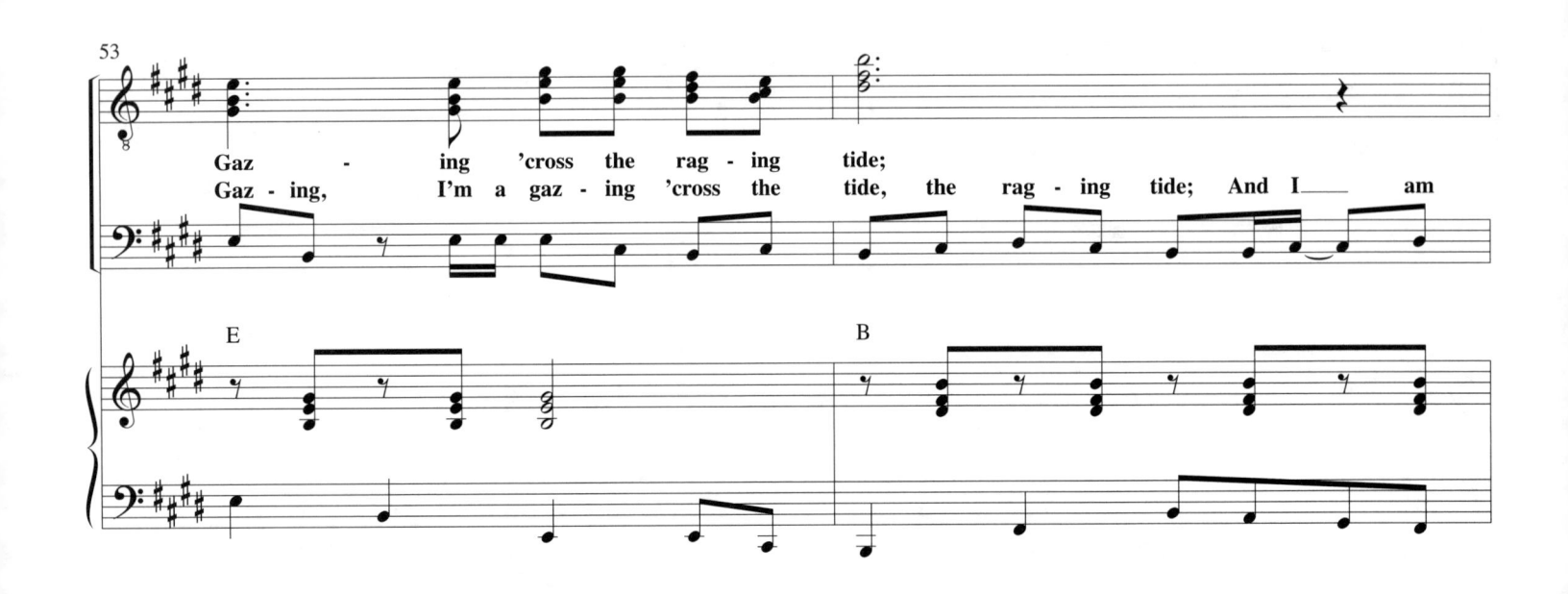

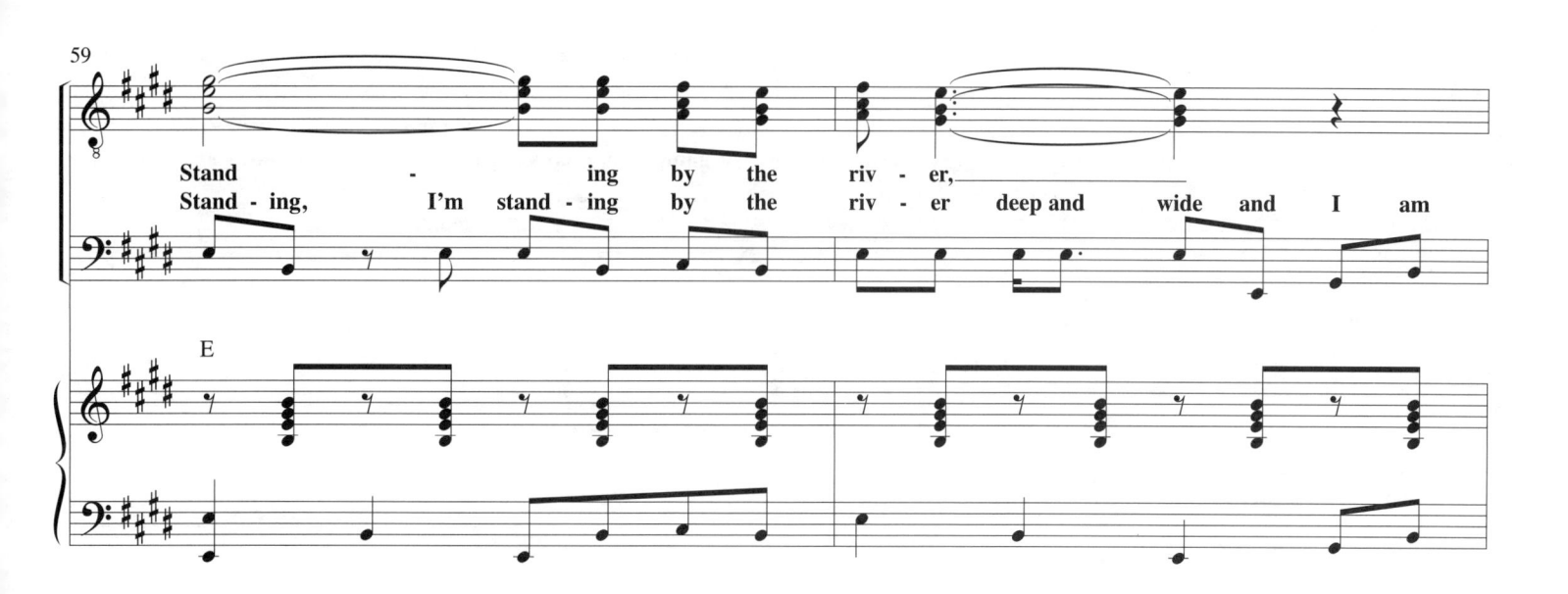

to get a glimpse of what's o - ver on the oth - er, Tryin'____ to get a glimpse of what's

o - ver
mel.
on the oth - er side!____
on the oth - er side, oth - er

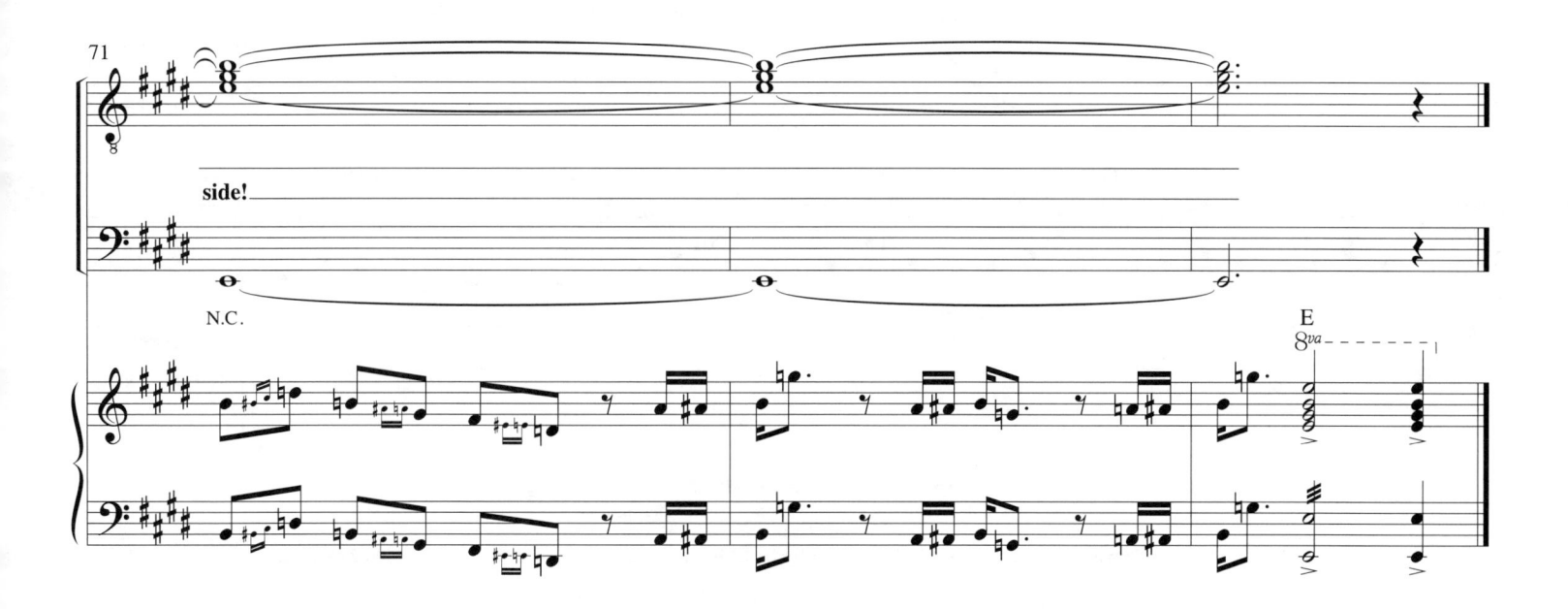

side!____

N.C.

This Could Be the Dawning of That Day

with

Until Then

Originally from the album "Great Love"

GLORIA GAITHER and
WILLIAM J. GAITHER

WILLIAM J. GAITHER

© 1971 William J. Gaither Music/ASCAP. All rights controlled by
Gaither Copyright Management. Used by permission.

PLEASE NOTE: Copying of this product is NOT covered by CCLI licenses. For CCLI information call 1-800-234-2446.

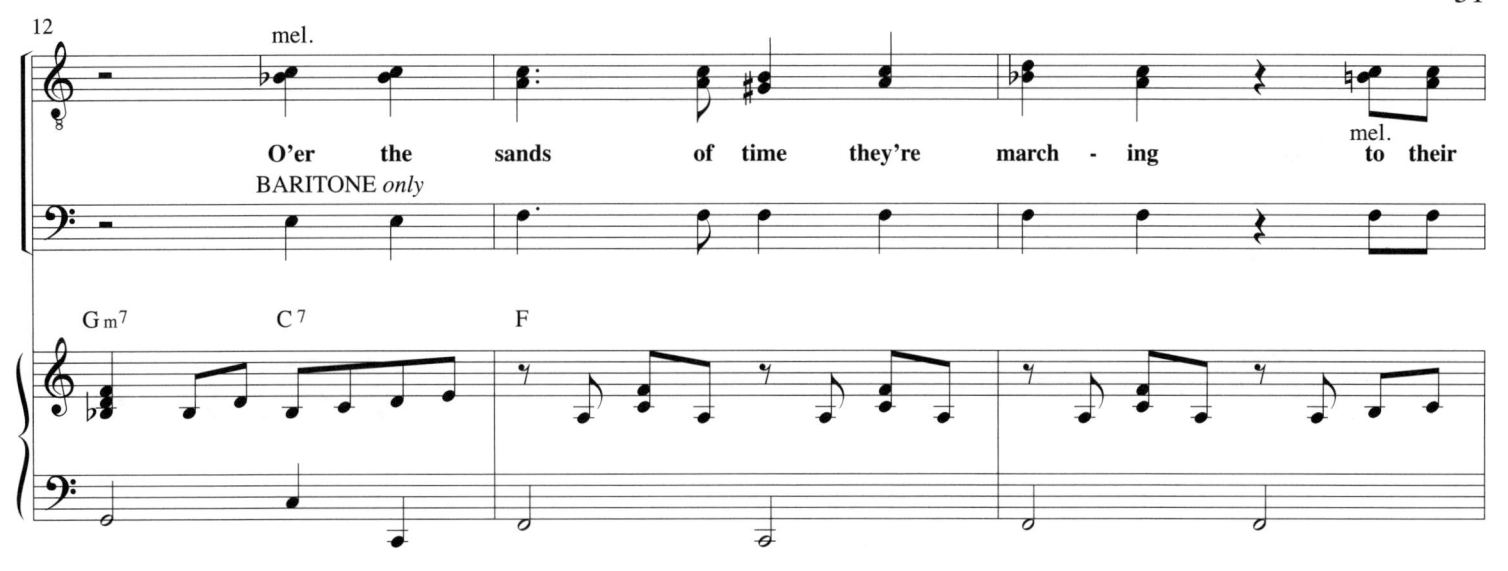

O'er the sands of time they're march - ing to their

King's great cor - o - na - tion, And this could be the

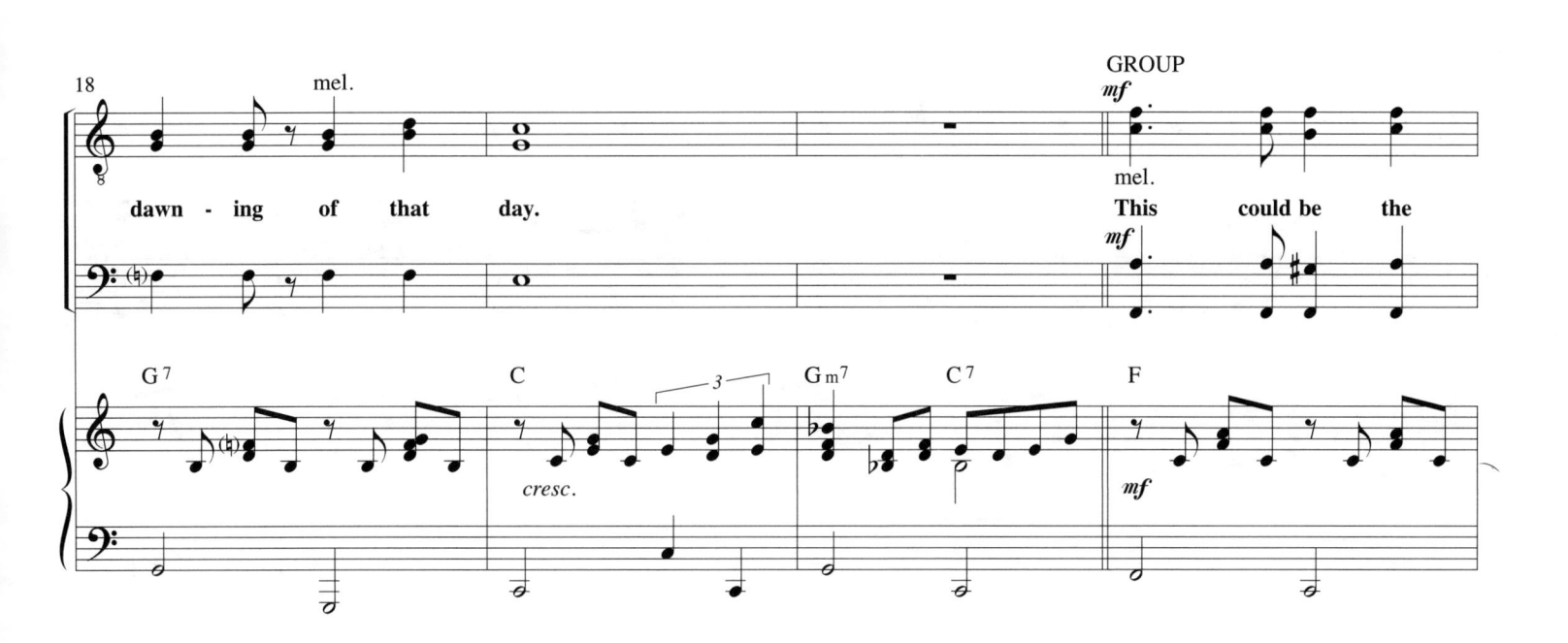

dawn - ing of that day. This could be the

dawn - ing   of that grand and glo - rious day;

F   D m⁷   C   D ⁷

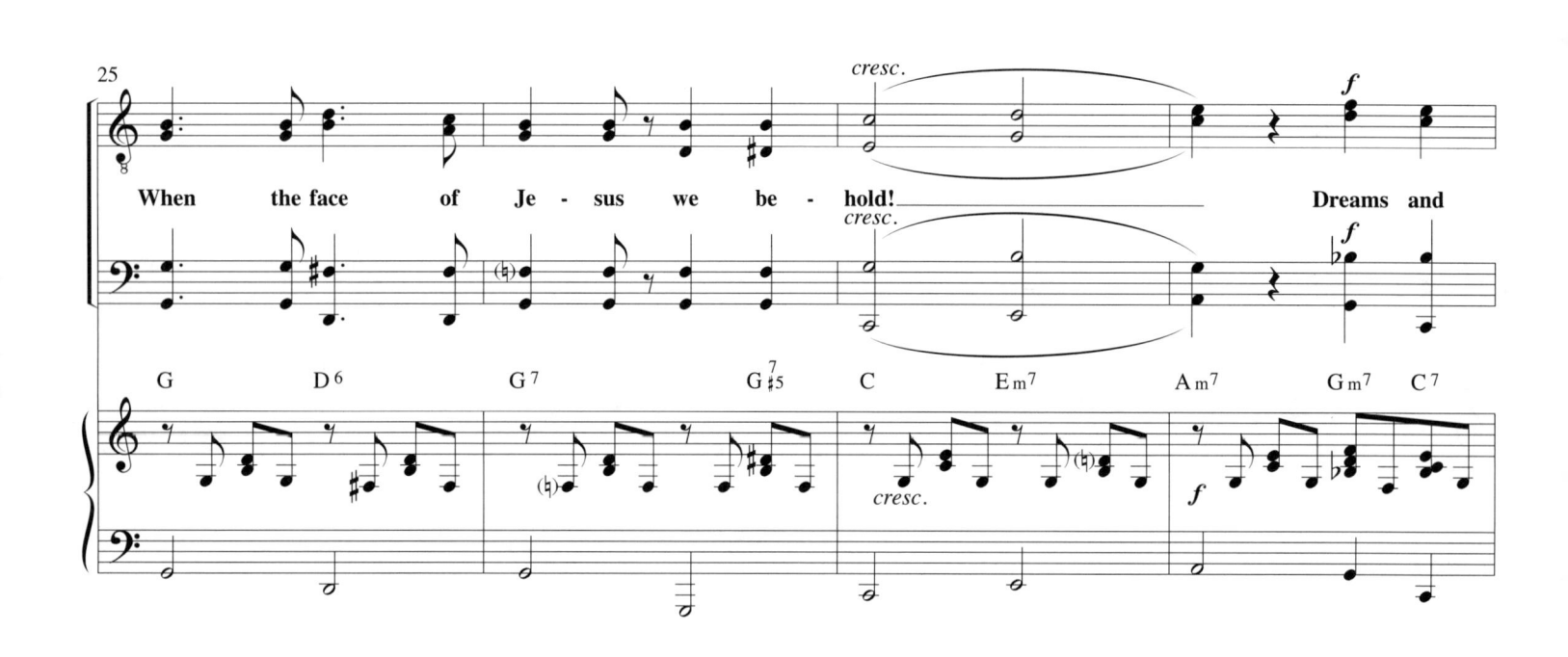

When the face of Je - sus we be - hold! _____ Dreams and

G   D ⁶   G ⁷   G♯⁷₅   C   E m⁷   A m⁷   G m⁷   C ⁷

hopes   of all   the a - ges   are a - wait - ing His re -

F   E m⁷

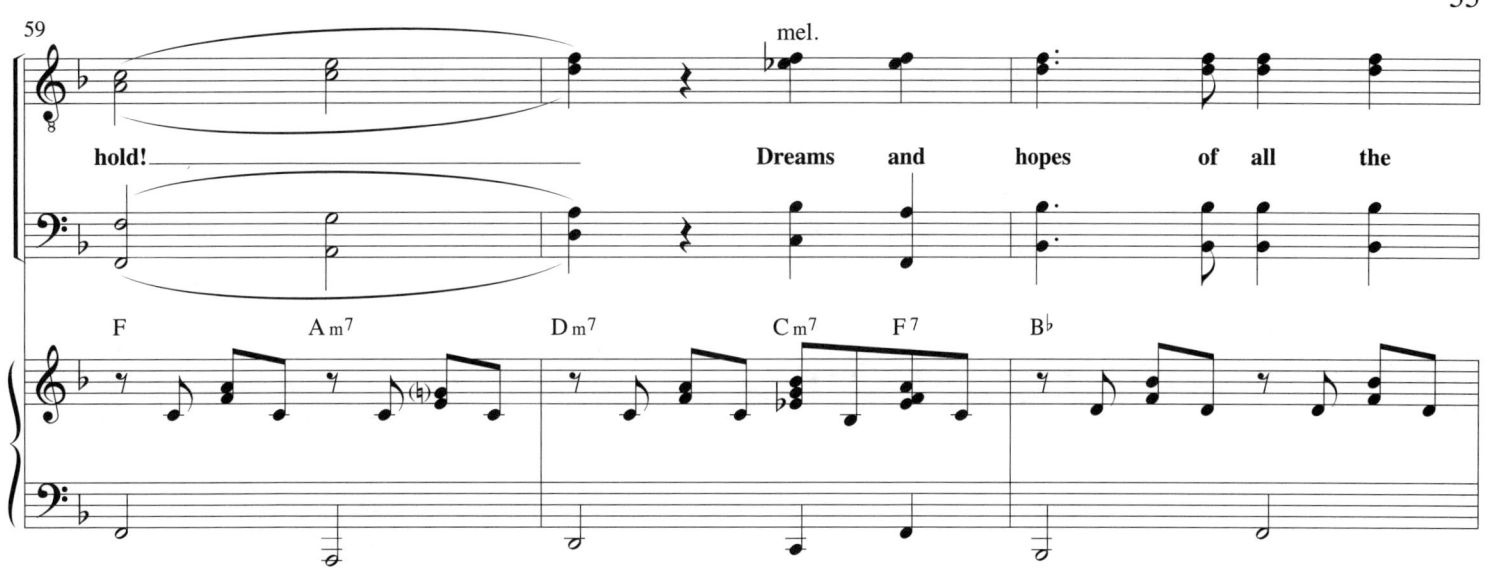

Dreams and hopes of all the

a - ges are a - wait - ing His re - turn - ing, And

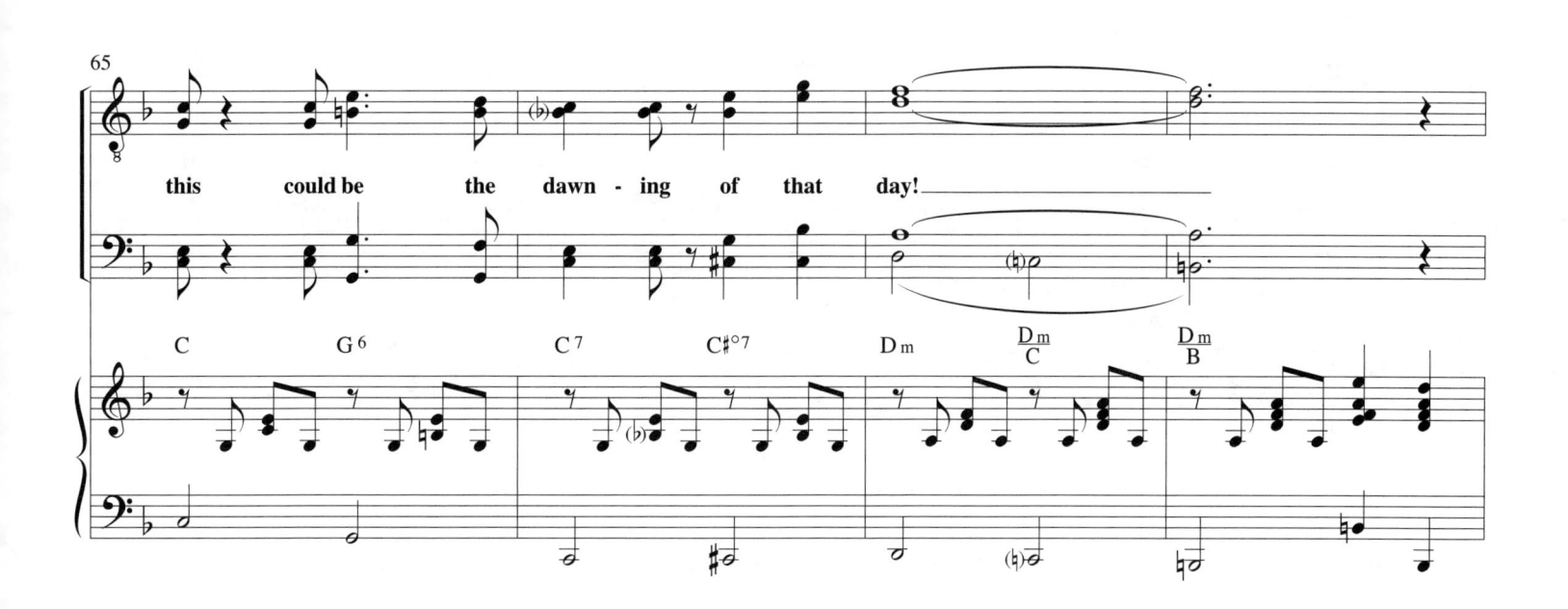

this could be the dawn - ing of that day!

56

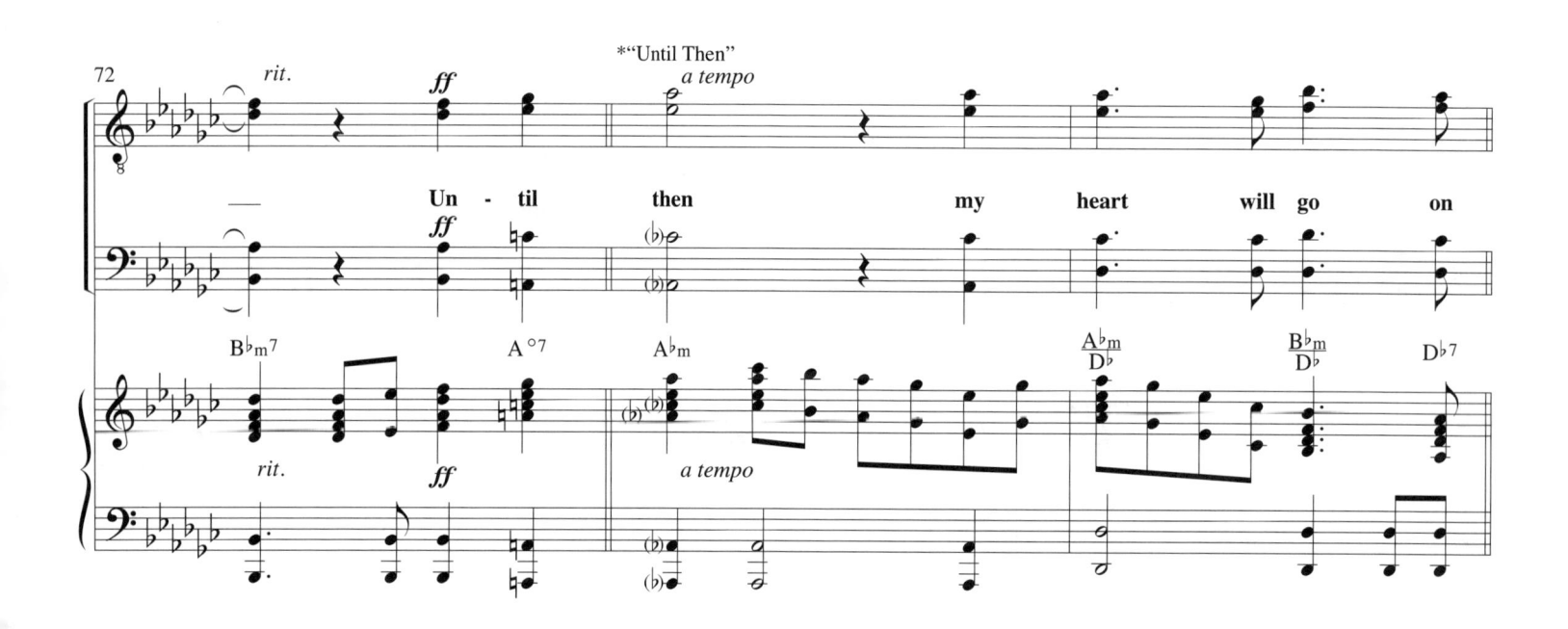

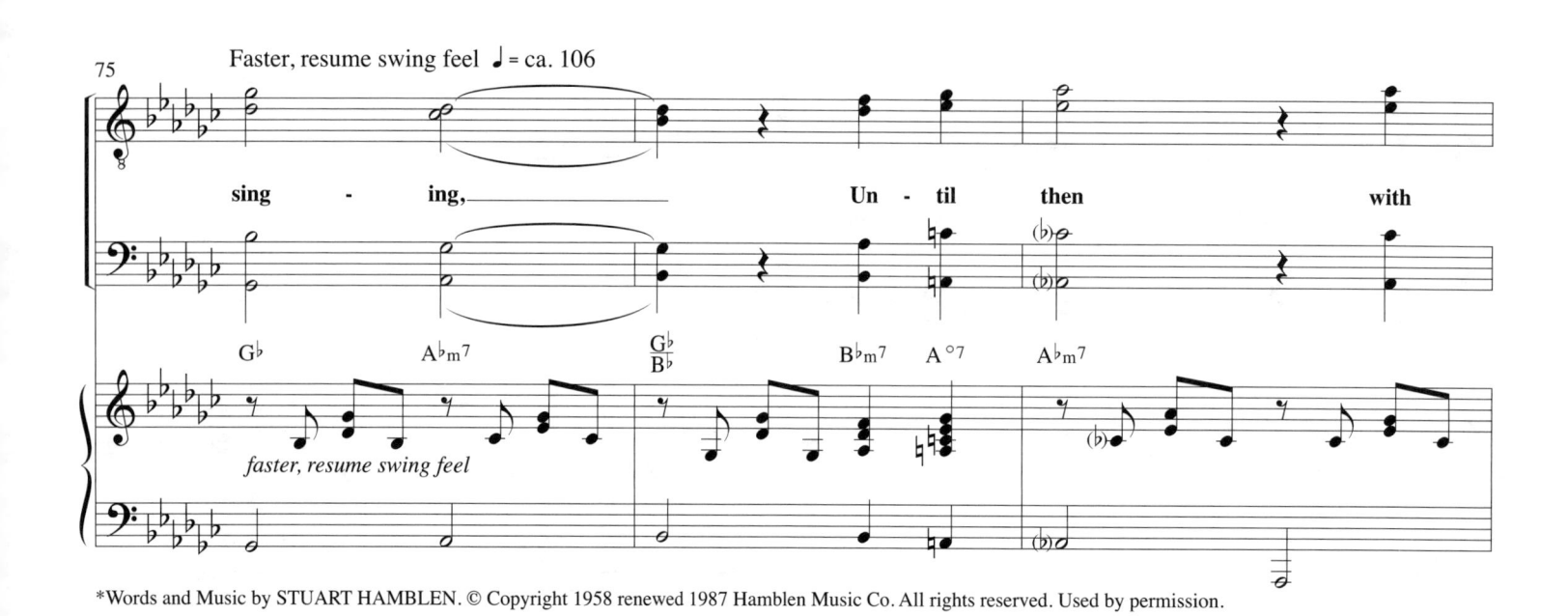

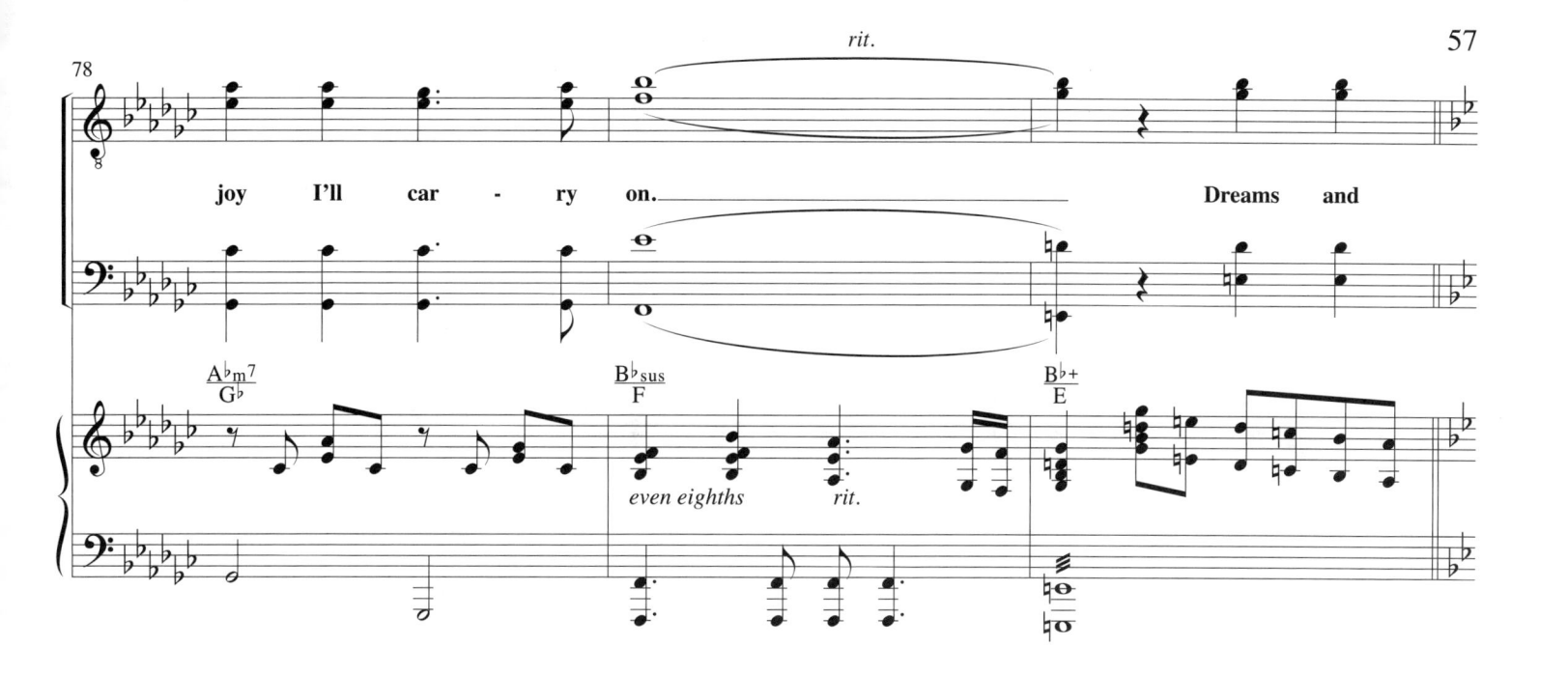

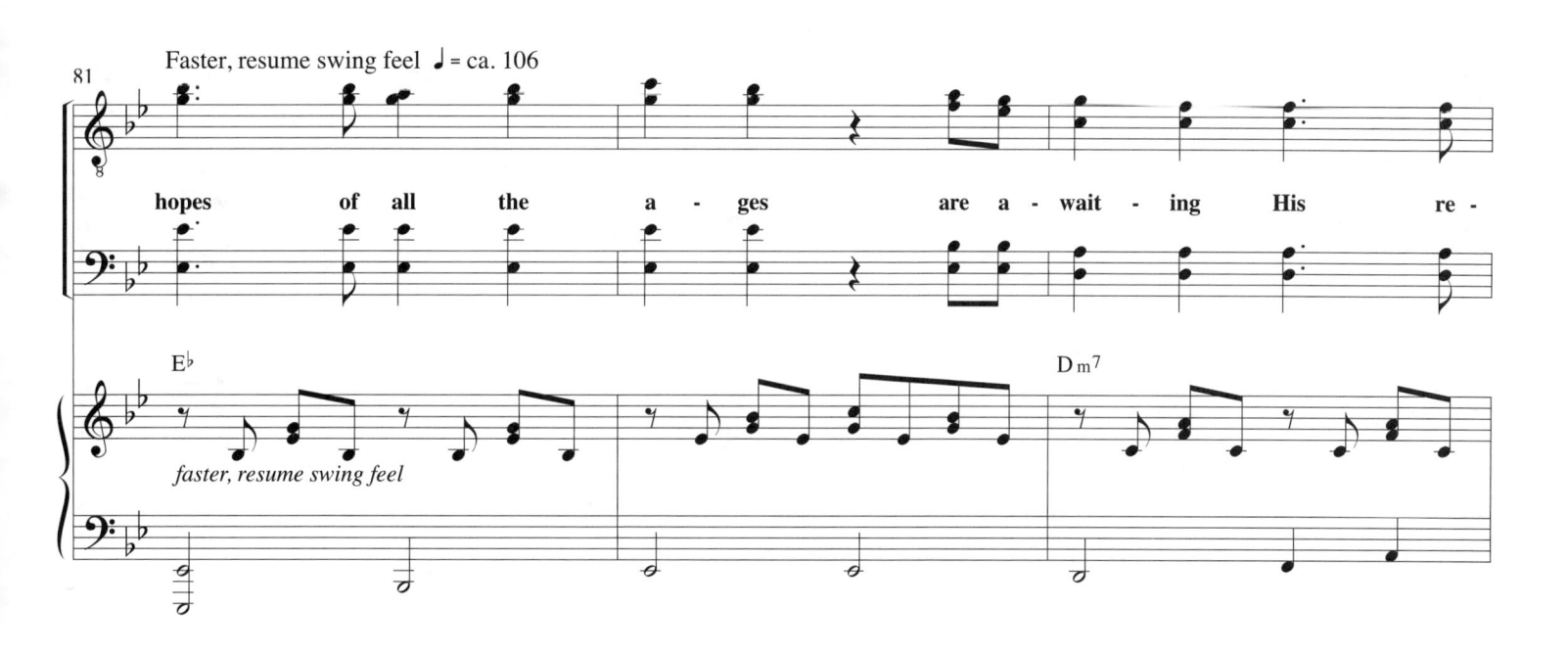

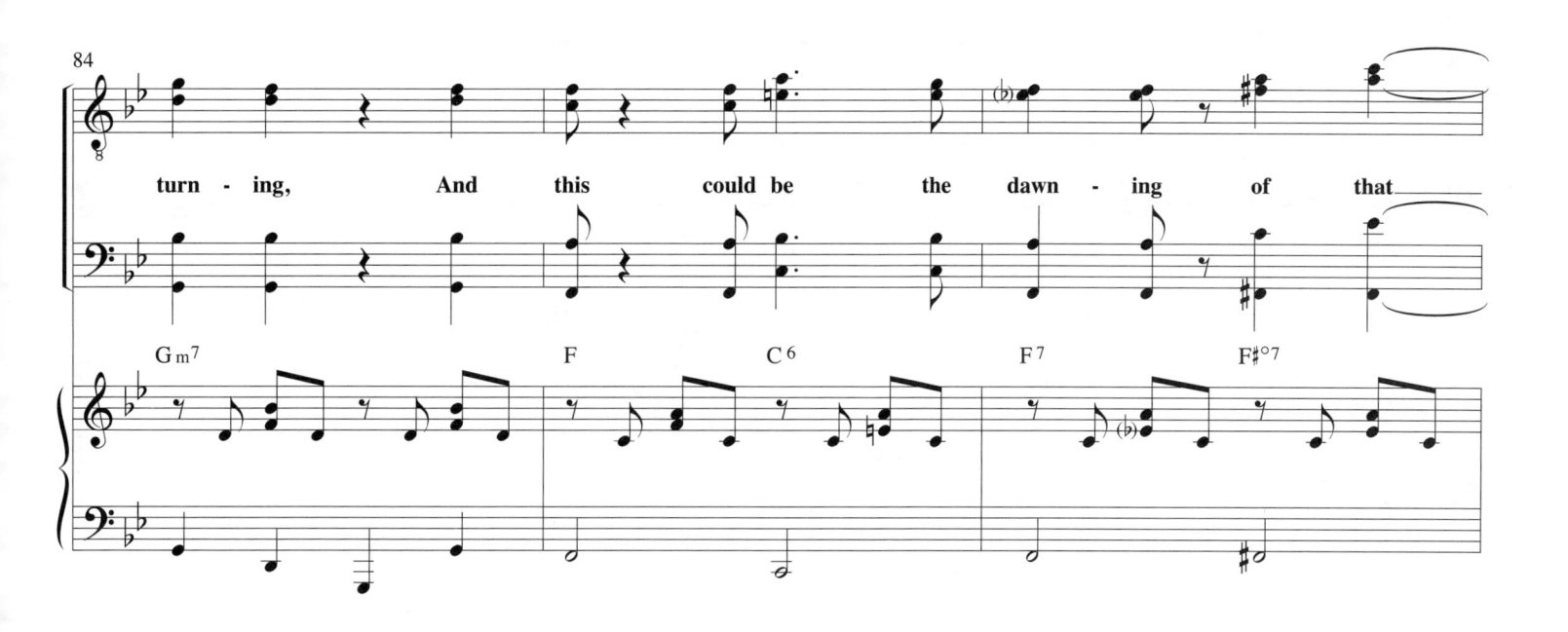

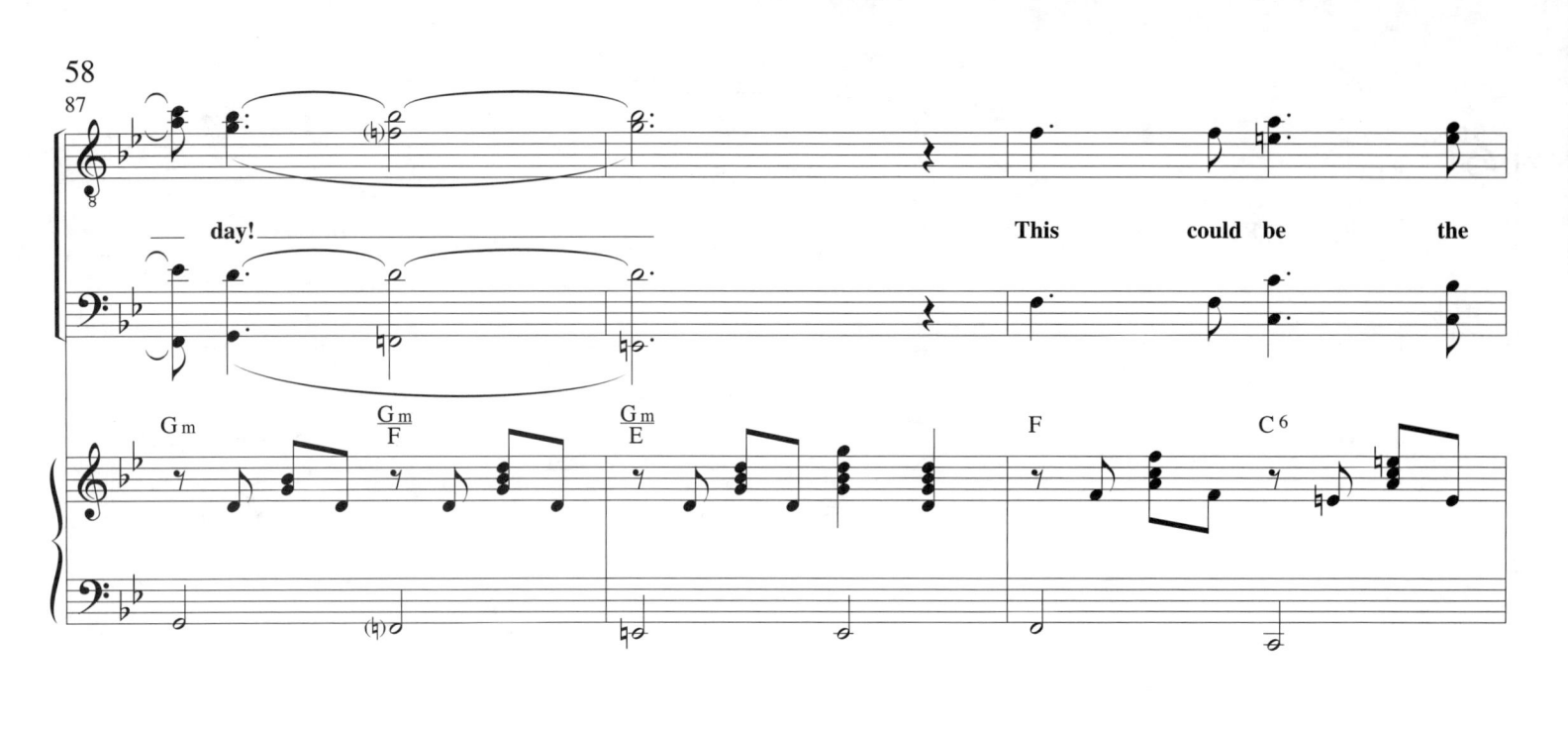

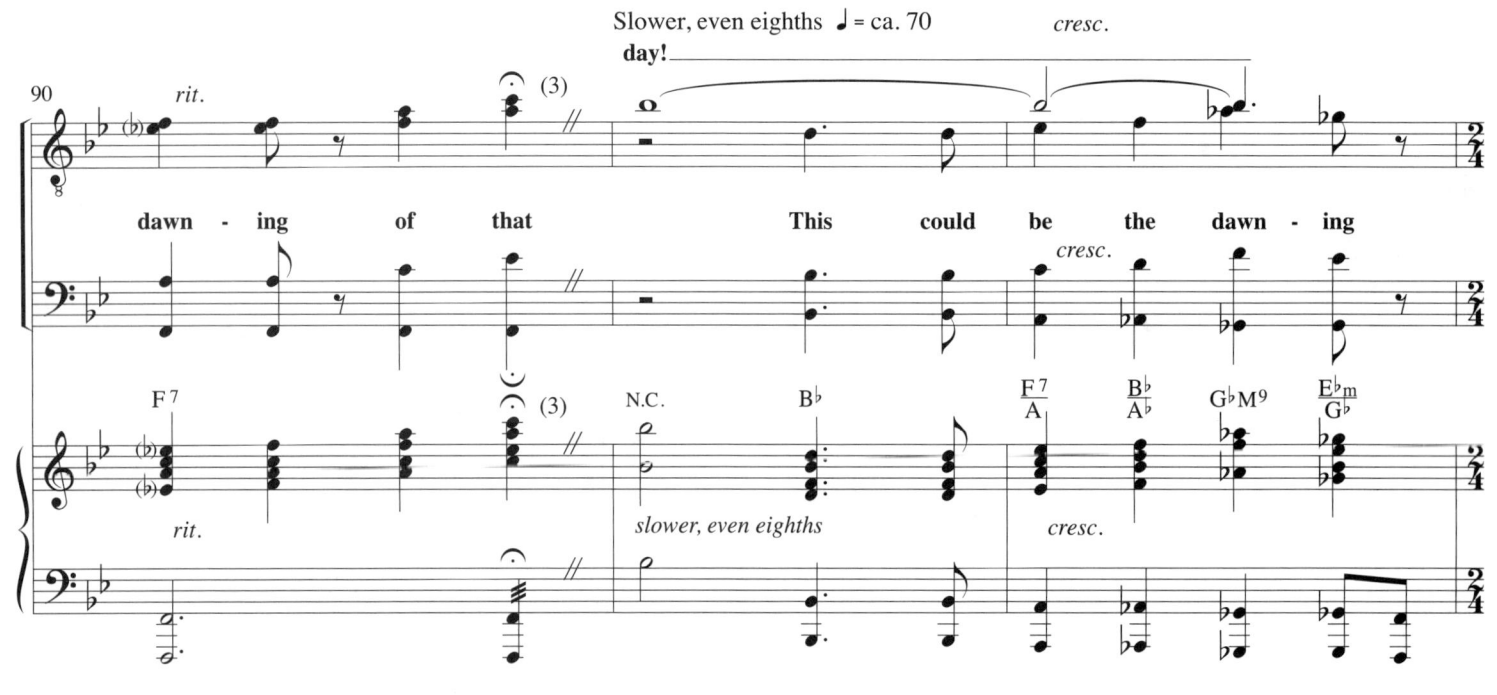

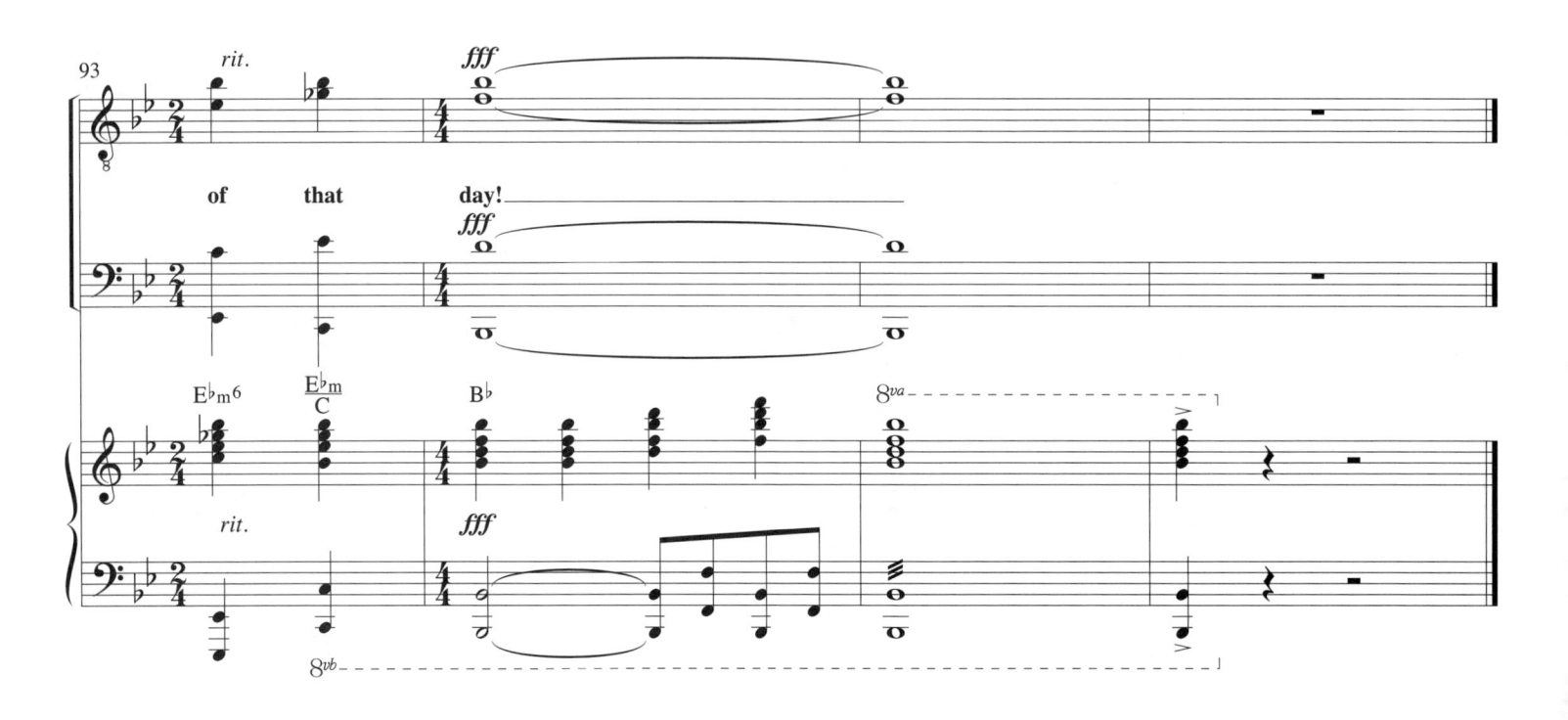

What a Savior*

Originally from the album "Get Away, Jordan"

Words and Music by
MARVIN P. DALTON

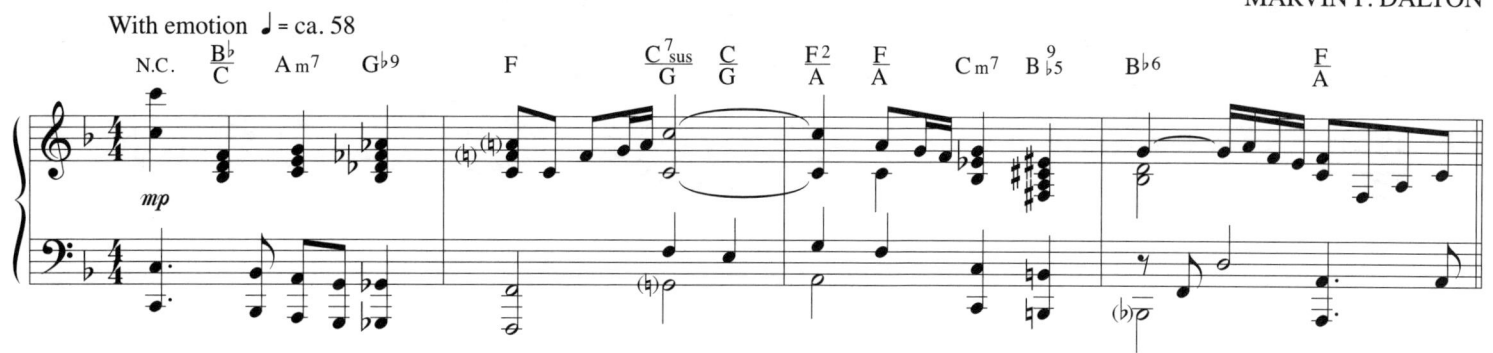

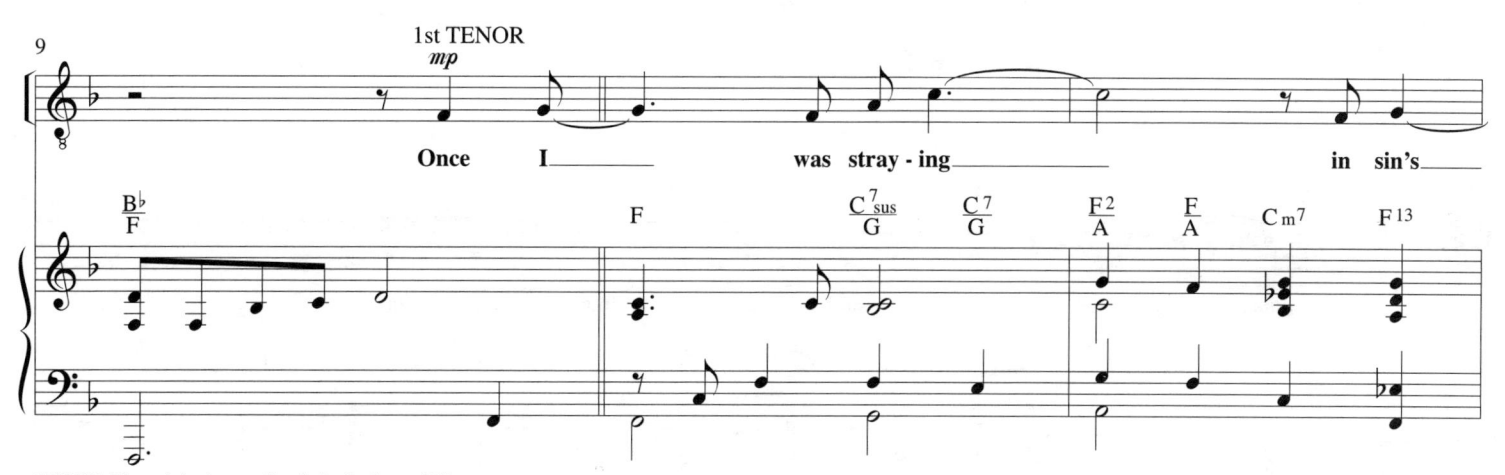

*NOTE: The original recording is in the key of Gb

O what a Sav - ior, O hal - le - lu - jah;

His heart was bro - ken on Cal - va -

ry. His hands were nail - scarred,

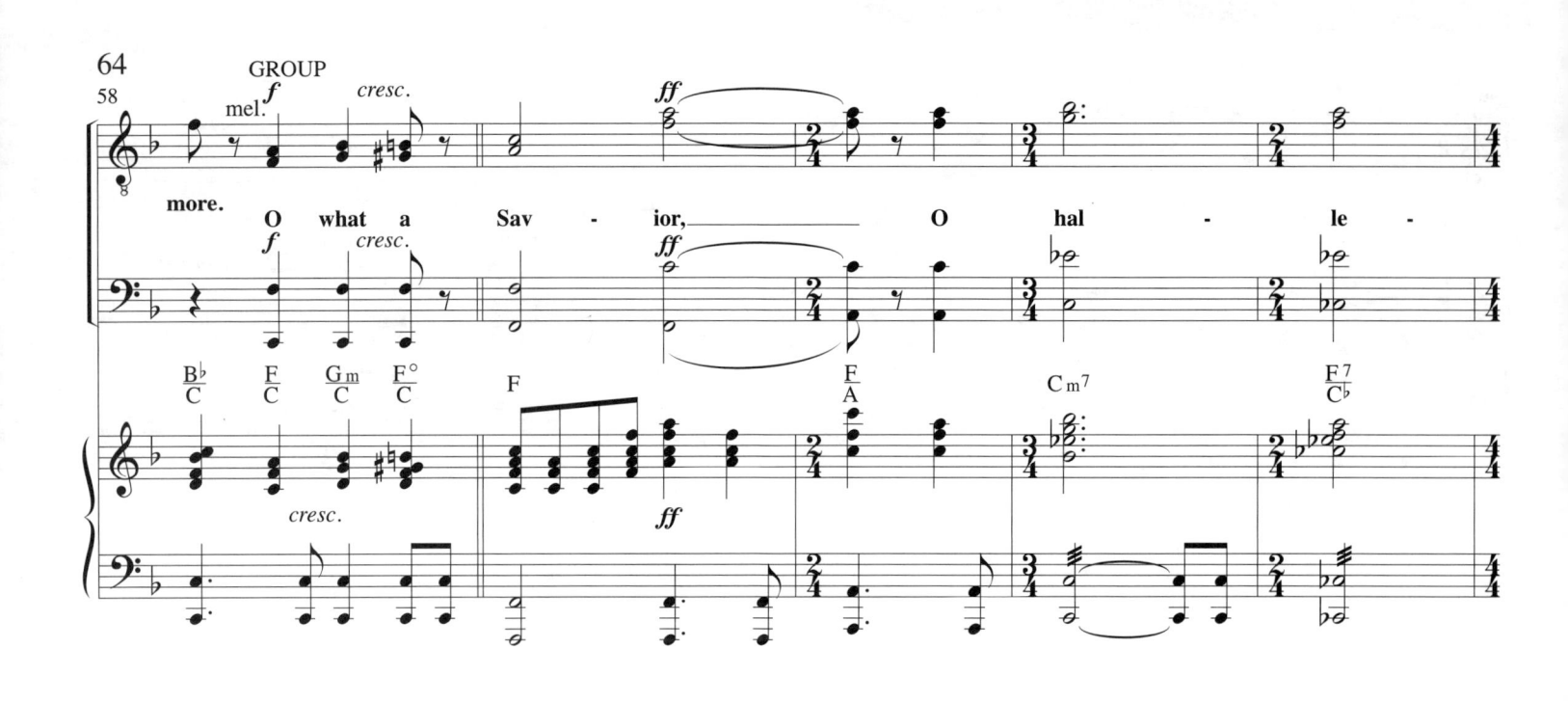

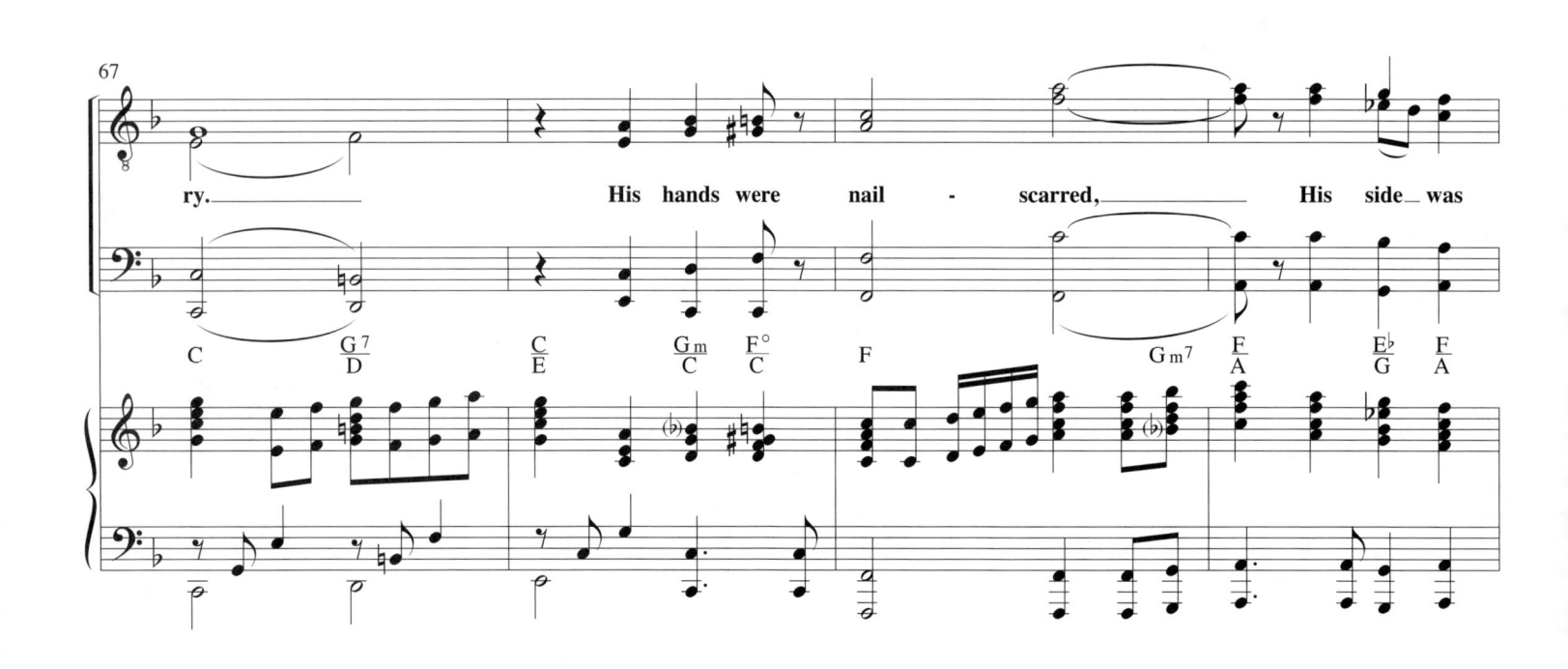

Wonderful Grace of Jesus

Originally from the album "Tribute to The Catheral Quartet"

Words and Music by
HALDOR LILLENAS
Arr. by Wayne Haun

With confidence ♩ = ca. 112

1. Won-der-ful grace of Je-sus, Great-er than all my sin— How shall my tongue de-scribe it? Where shall His praise be-gin? Tak-ing a-way my bur-den, Set-ting my spir-it free; For the
2. Won-der-ful grace of Je-sus, Reach-ing the most de-filed— By His trans-form-ing pow-er Mak-ing him God's dear child, Pur-chas-ing peace and heav-en For all e-ter-ni-ty; For the

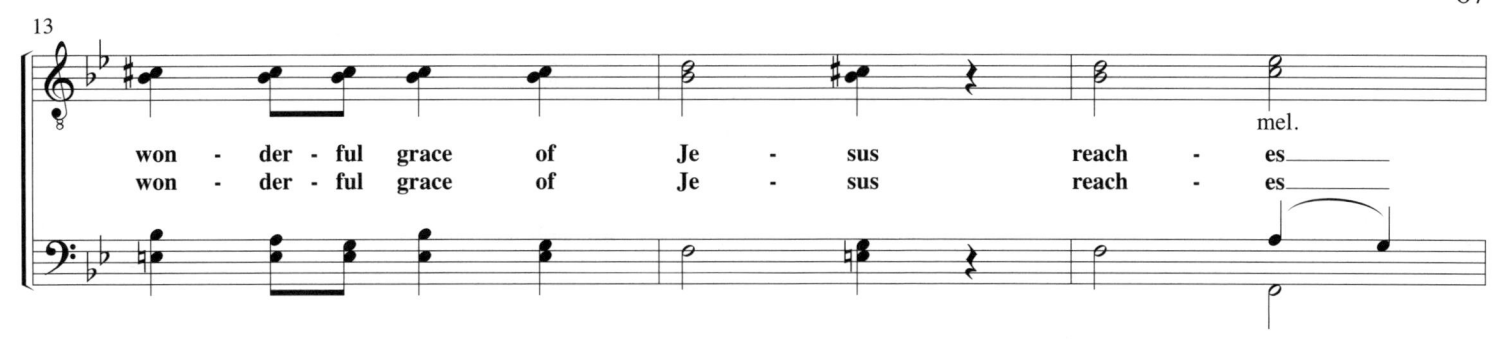

wonderful grace of Jesus reaches_____ mel.
wonderful grace of Jesus reaches_____

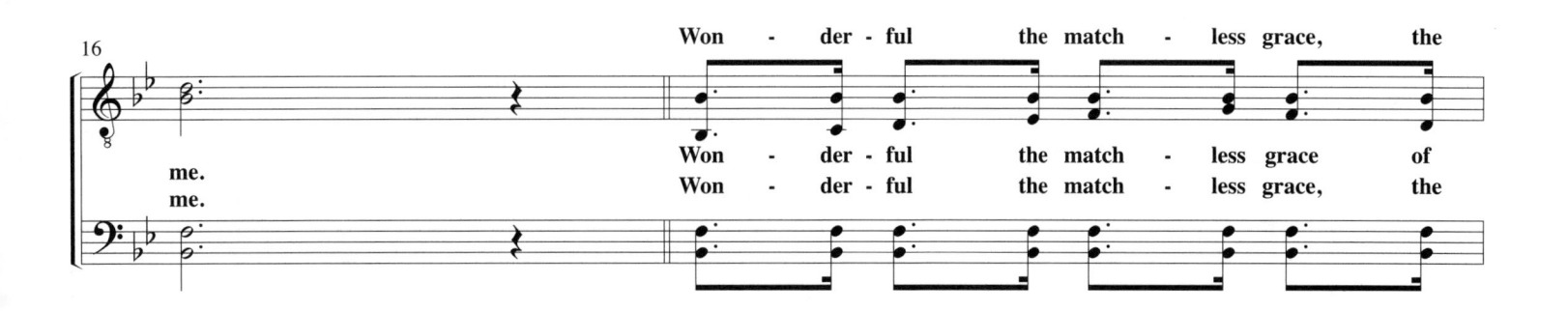

Wonderful the matchless grace, the
me.
Wonderful the matchless grace of
me.
Wonderful the matchless grace, the

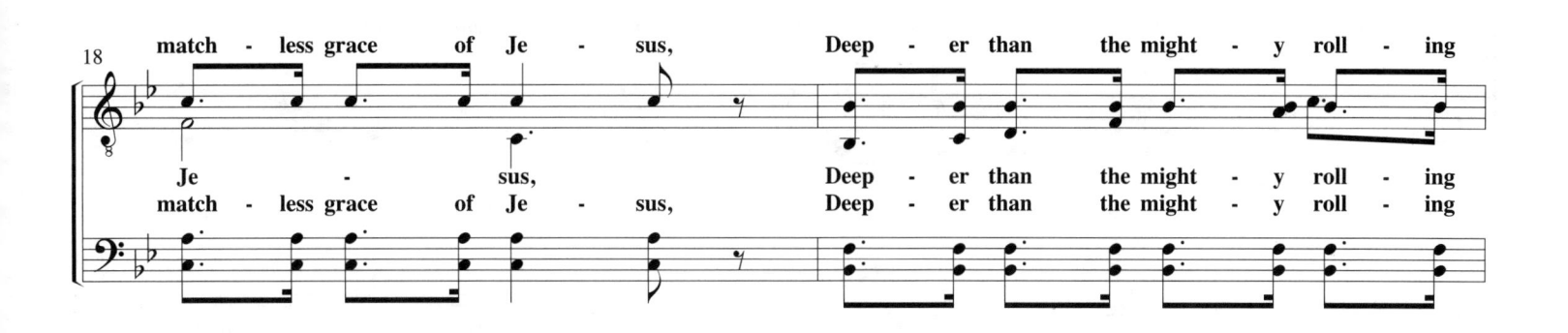

matchless grace of Jesus, Deeper than the mighty rolling
Je - sus, Deeper than the mighty rolling
matchless grace of Jesus, Deeper than the mighty rolling

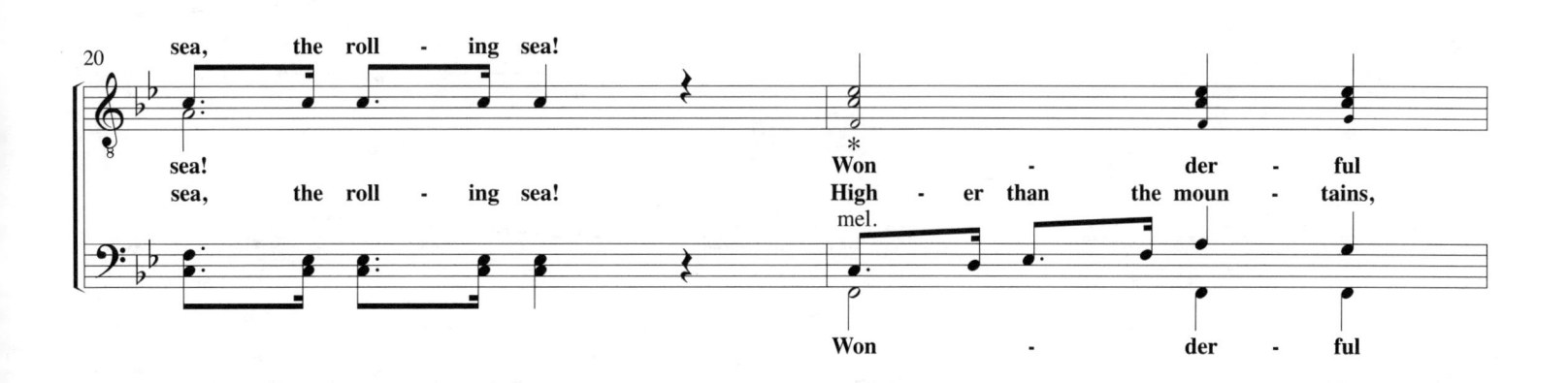

sea, the rolling sea!
sea!
*Wonderful
sea, the rolling sea! Higher than the mountains,
mel.
Wonderful

grace, all - suf - fi - cient for
Sparkling like a fountain, All - suf - fi - cient grace for ev - en
grace, all - suf - fi - cient for

*Optional 5th part (cued notes)

Until We Fly Away

Originally from the album "Get Away, Jordan"

Words and Music by
JOEL LINDSEY and PAM THUM

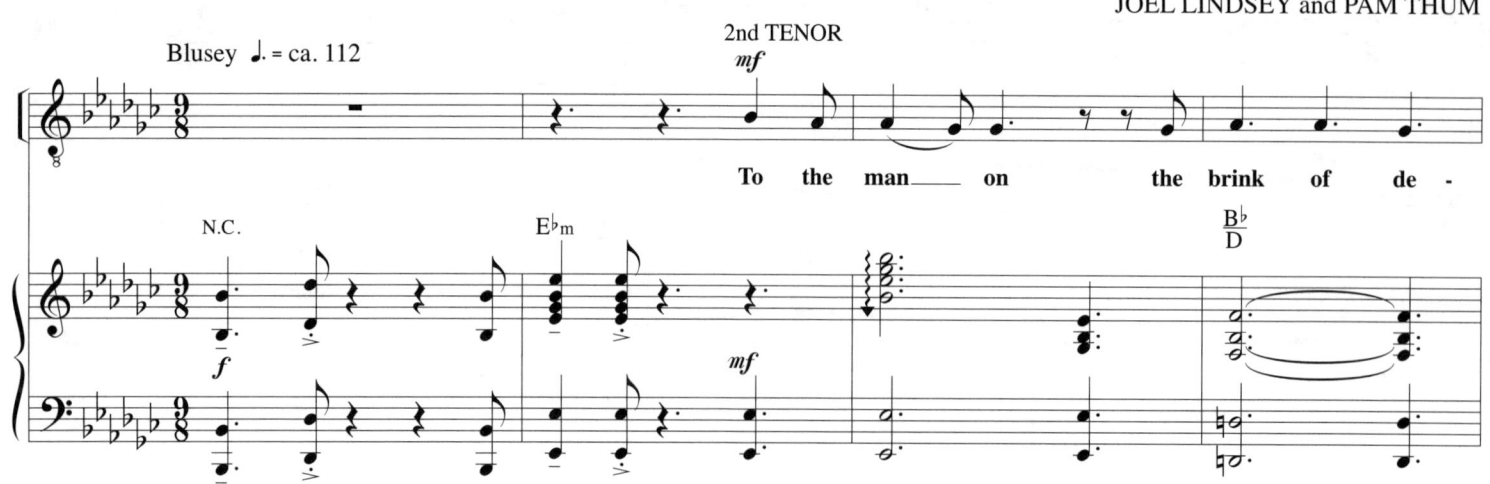

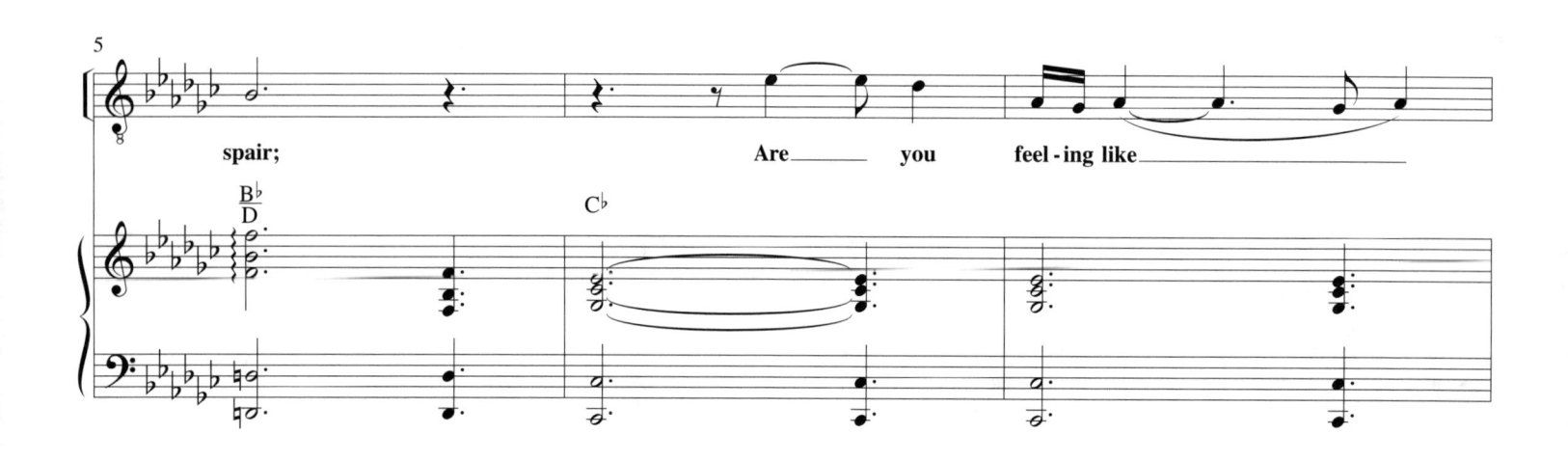

PLEASE NOTE: Copying of this product is NOT covered by CCLI licenses. For CCLI information call 1-800-234-2446.

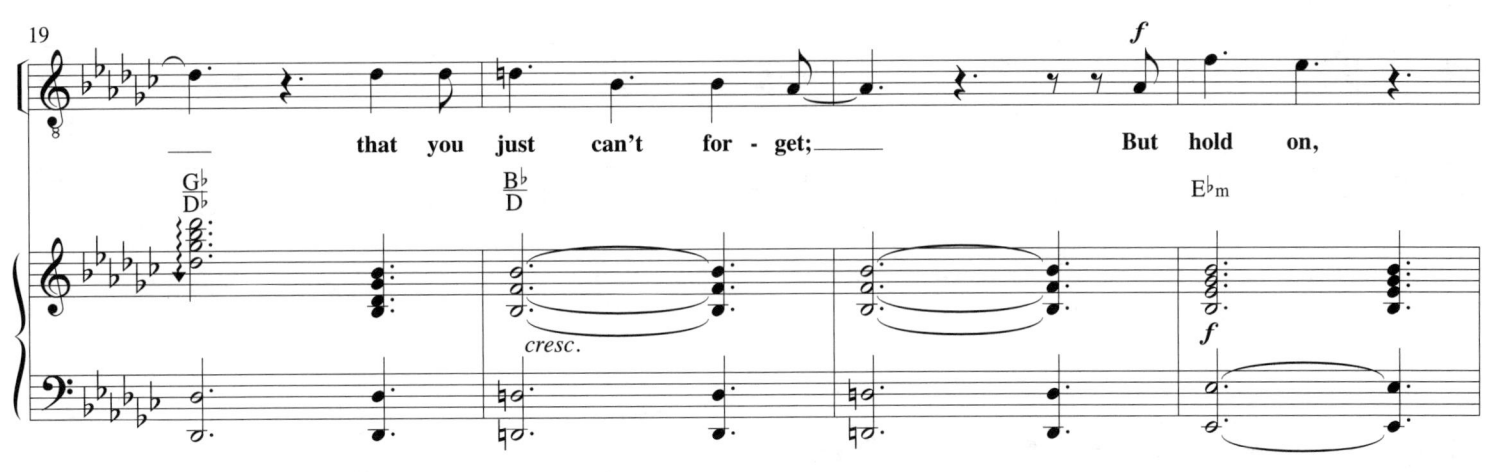

72

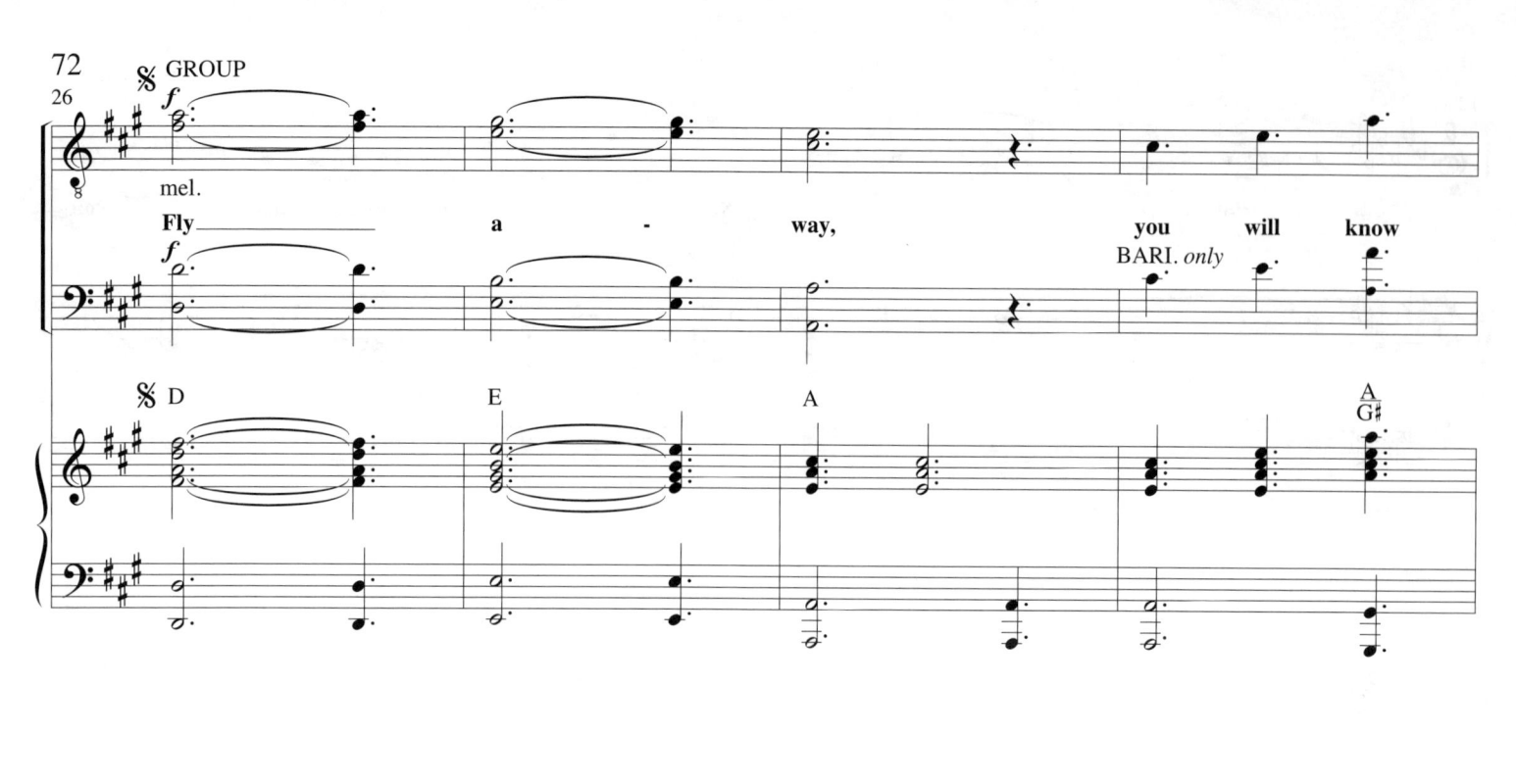

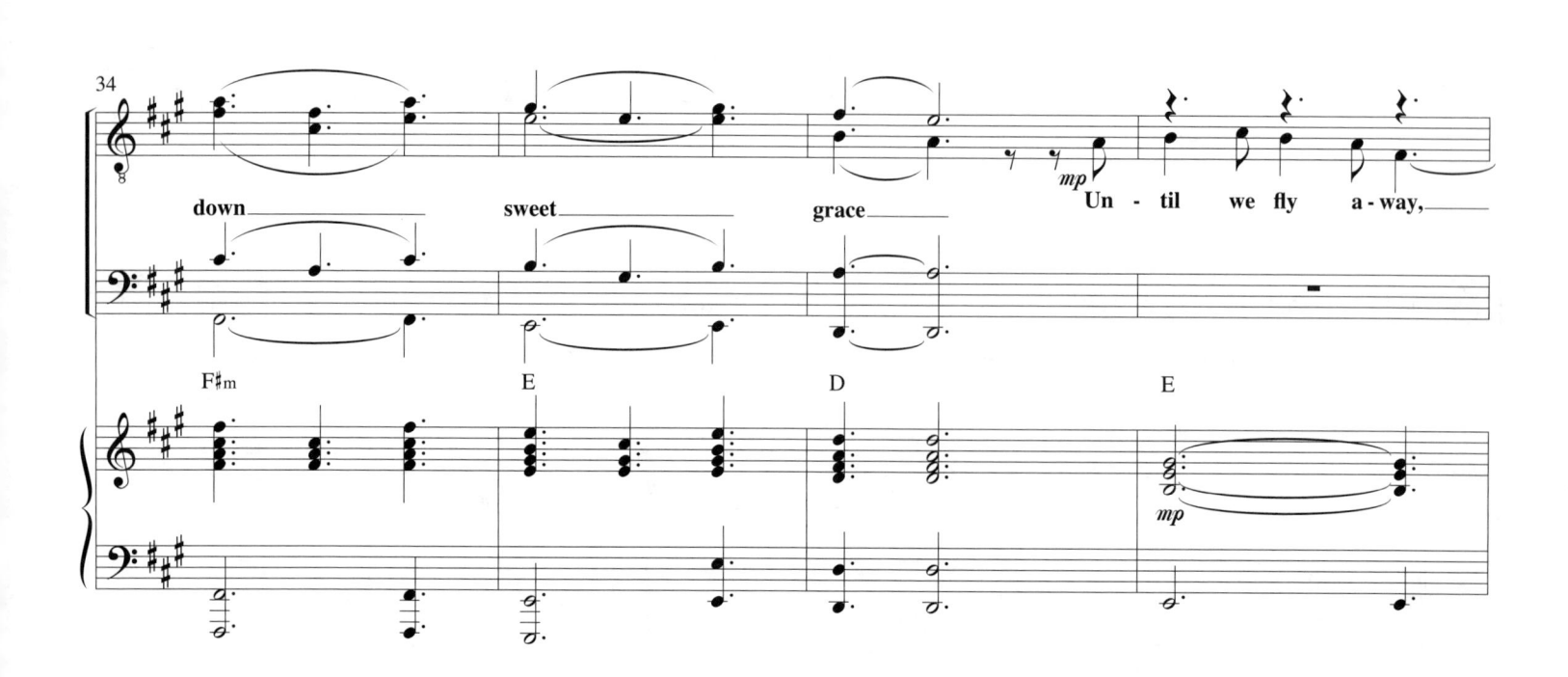

lost,_____ Nurs - ing__ the wounds from____ the bat - tles__ you've

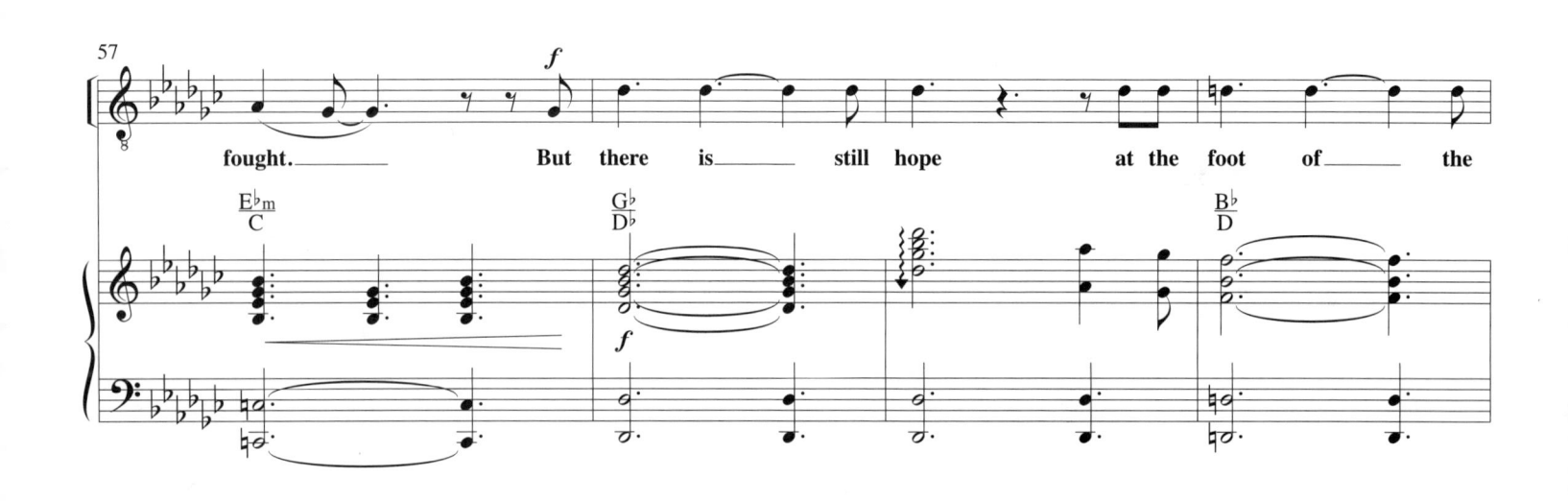

fought._____ But there is___ still hope at the foot of___ the

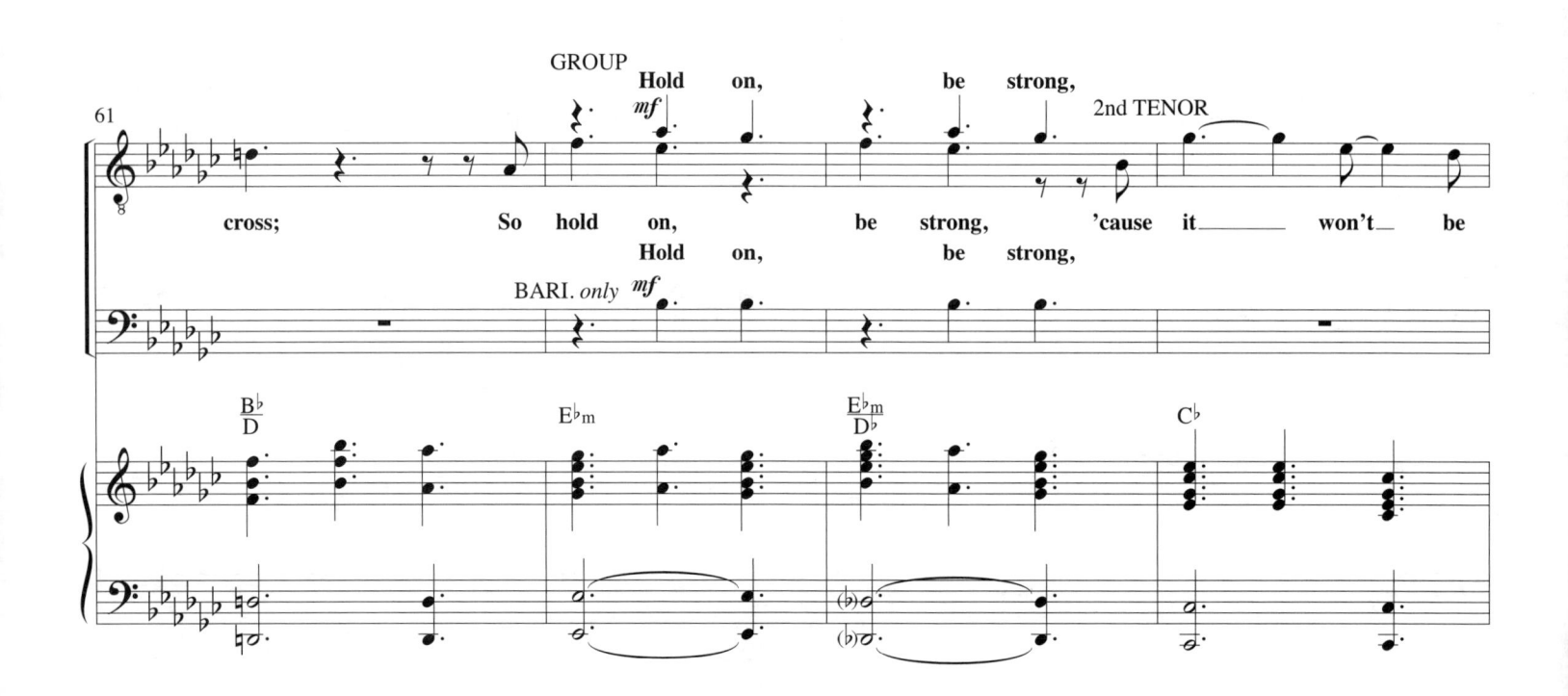

GROUP
Hold on, be strong,
2nd TENOR

cross; So hold on, be strong, 'cause it___ won't__ be
Hold on, be strong,

BARI. only

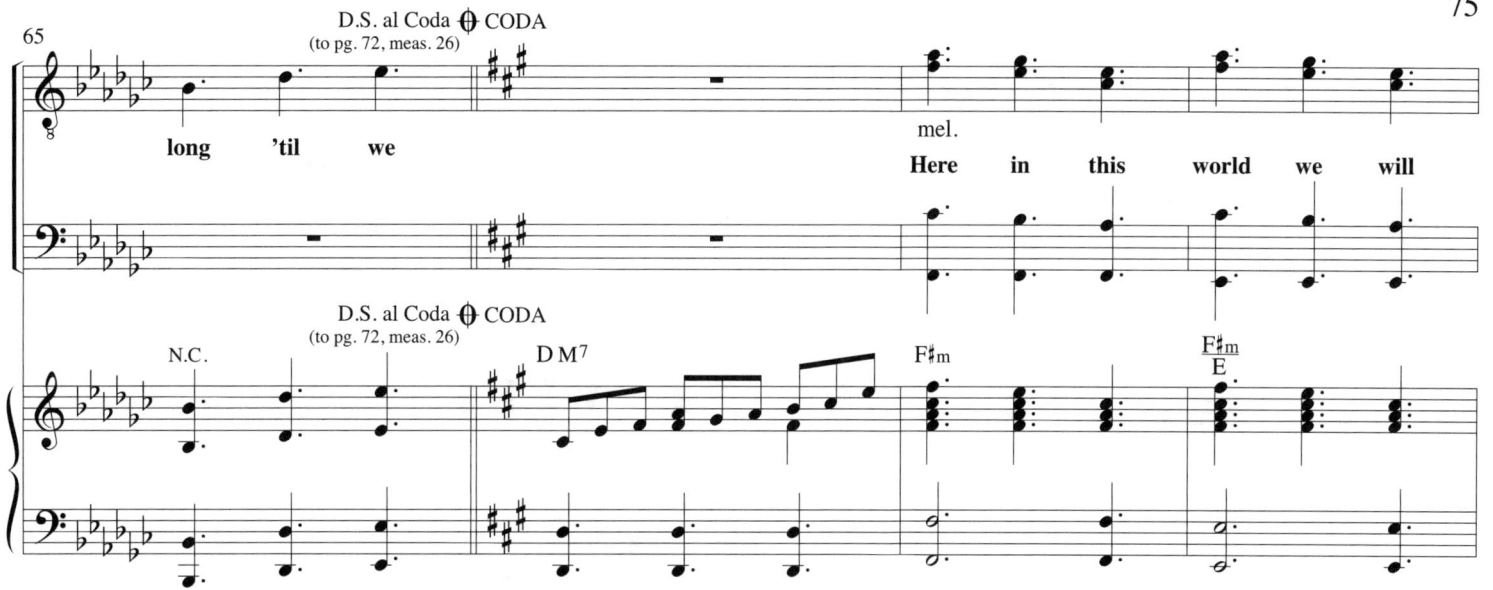

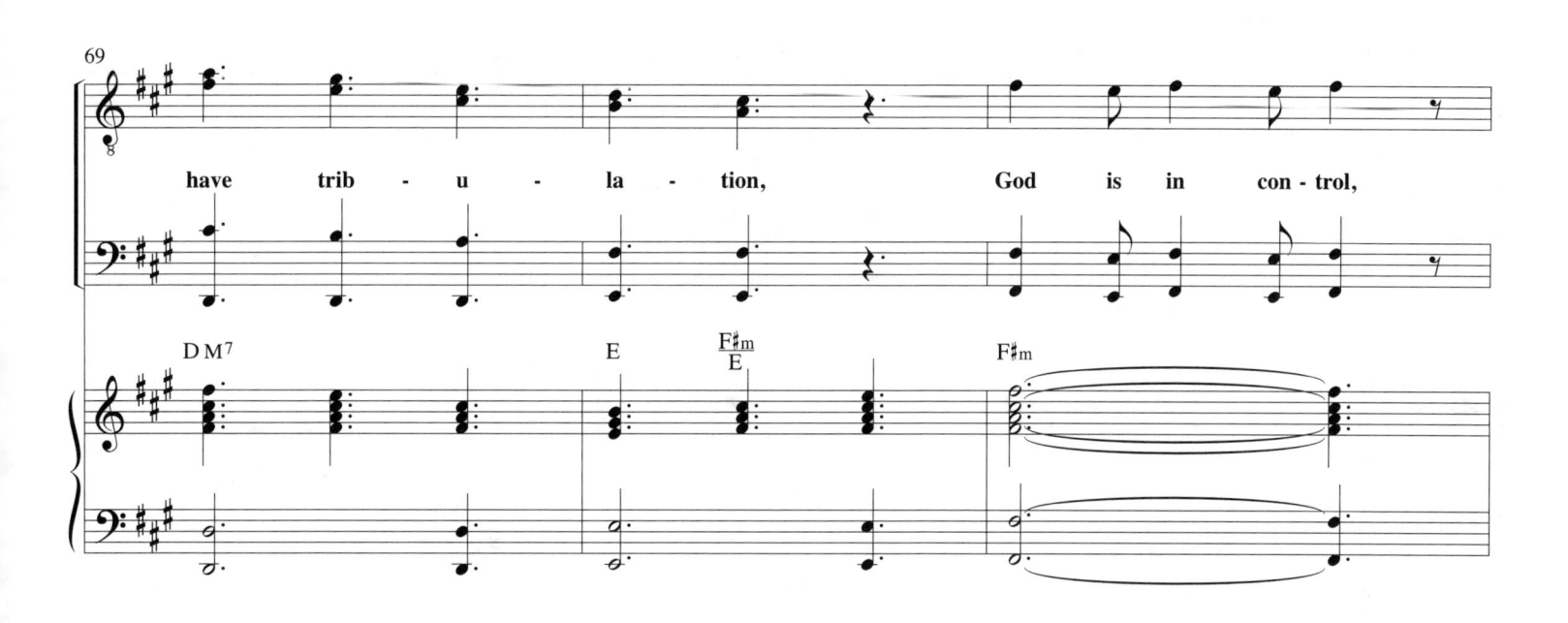

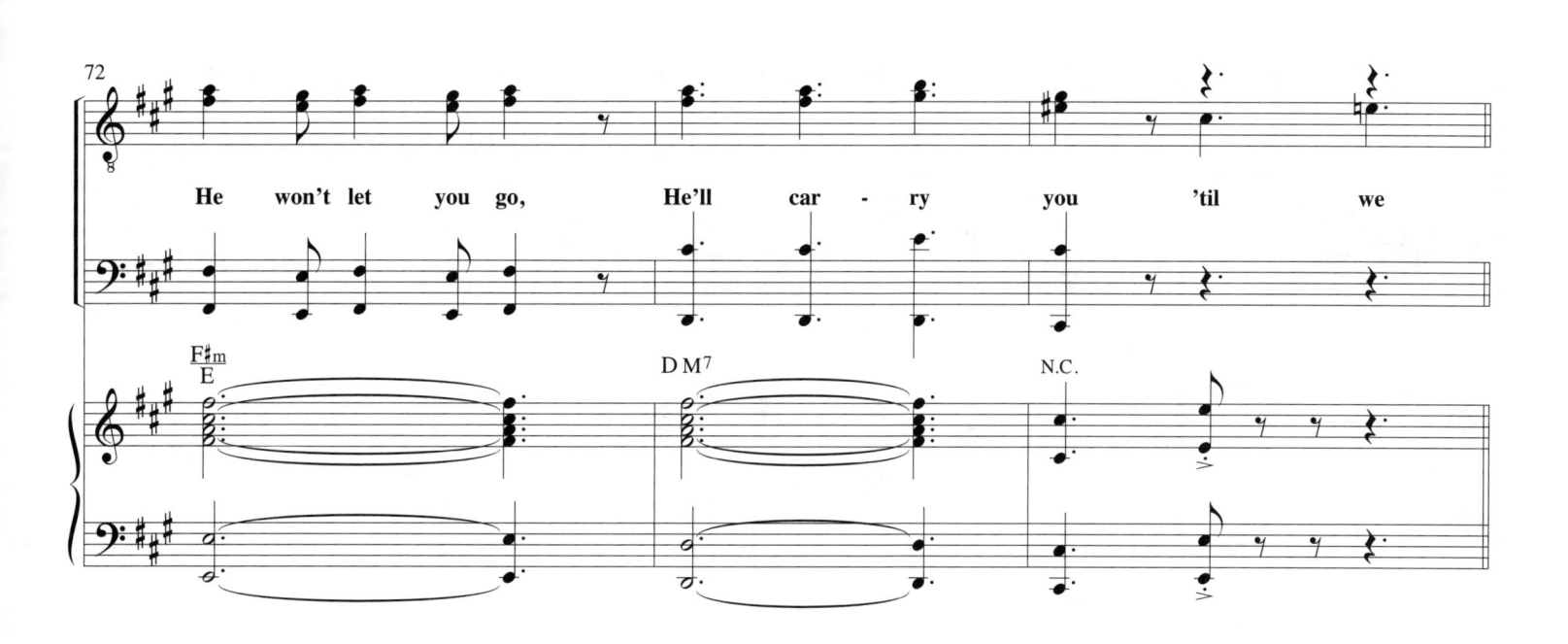

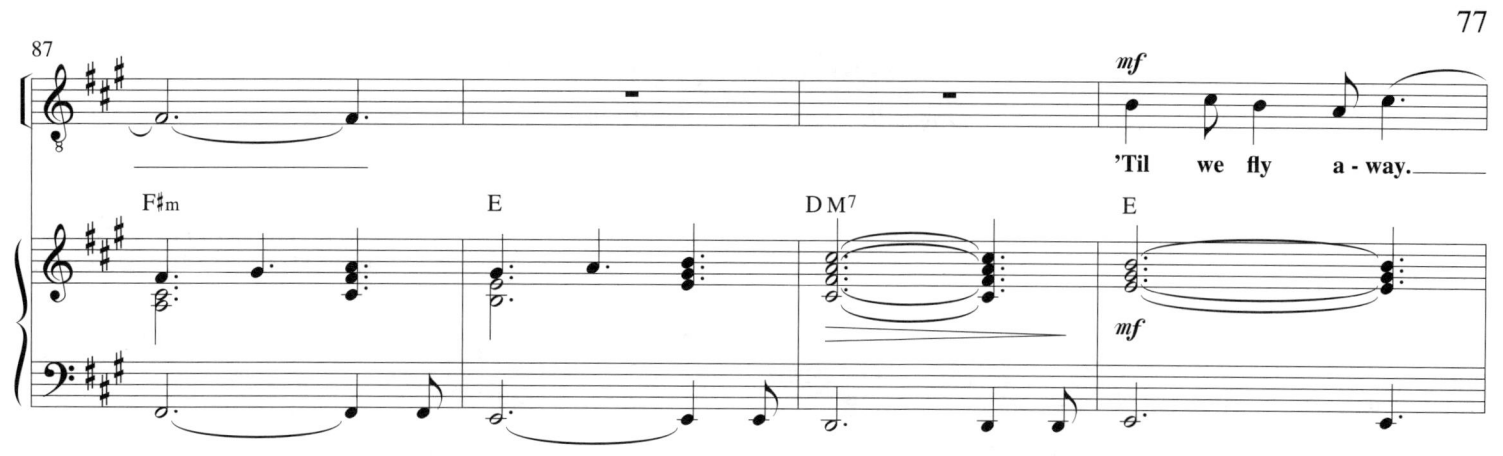

'Til we fly a - way.___

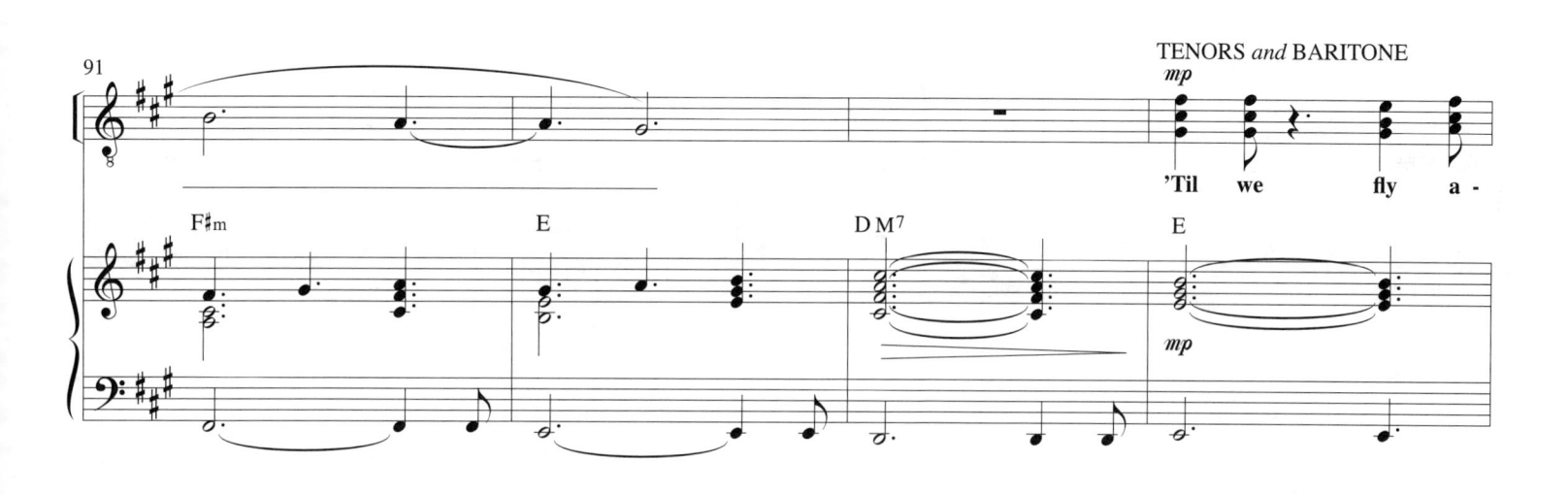

TENORS *and* BARITONE

'Til we fly a -

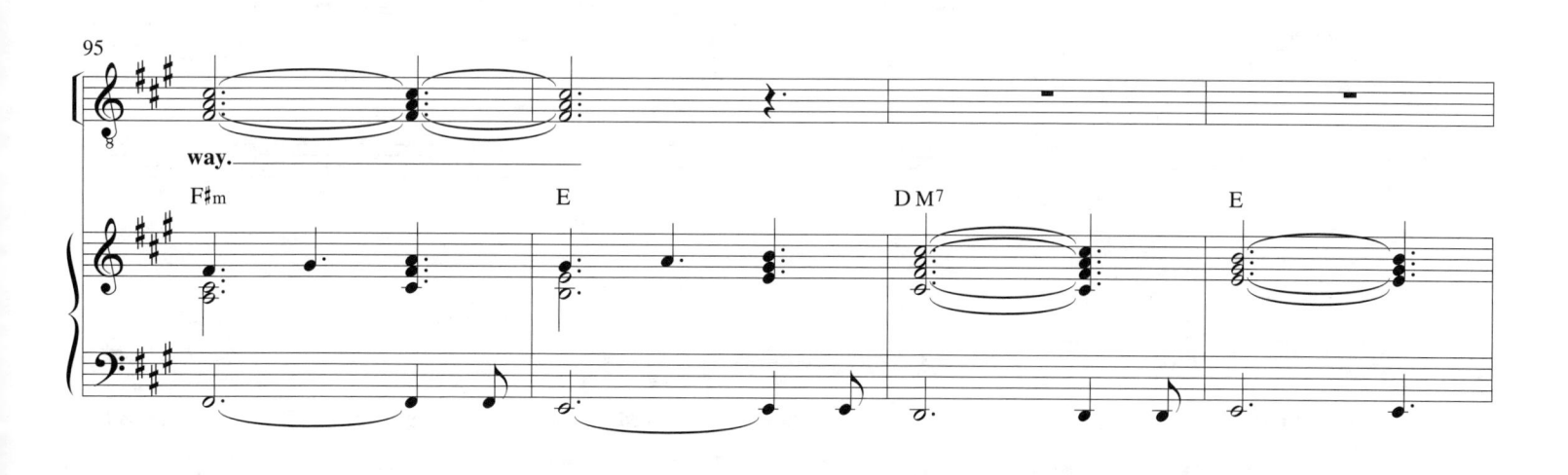

way.___

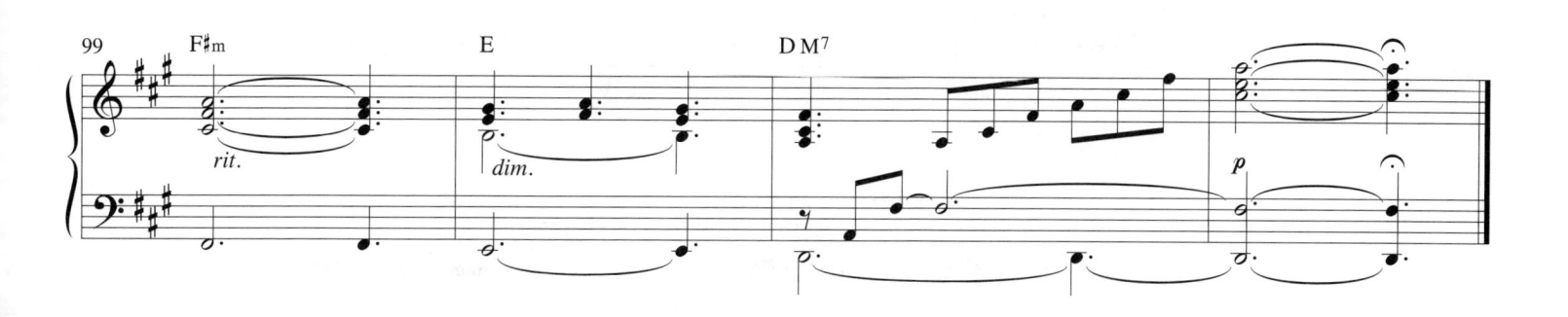

Forgiven Again

Originally from the album "Self Titled"

Words and Music by
GLORIA GAITHER and
WILLIAM BENJAMIN GAITHER

I left my fam-'ly, the love I had known, I could-n't be-lieve how cal-loused I'd grown; Then I

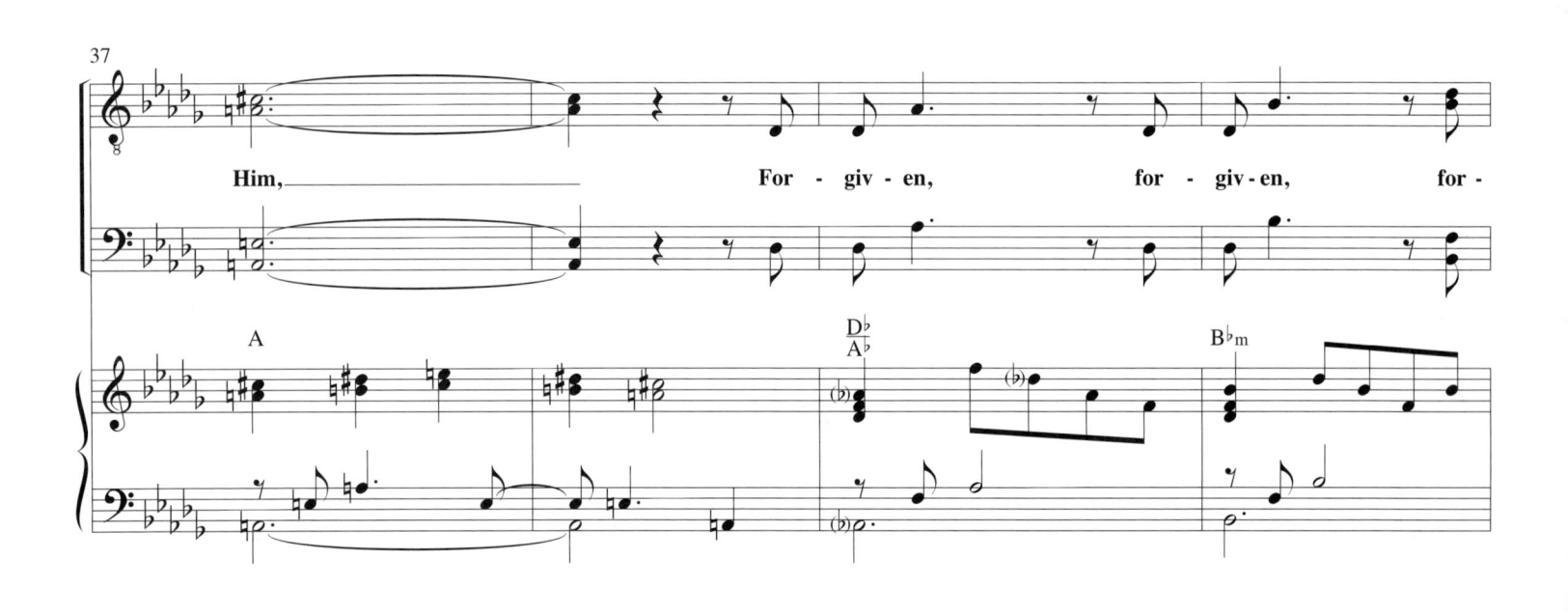

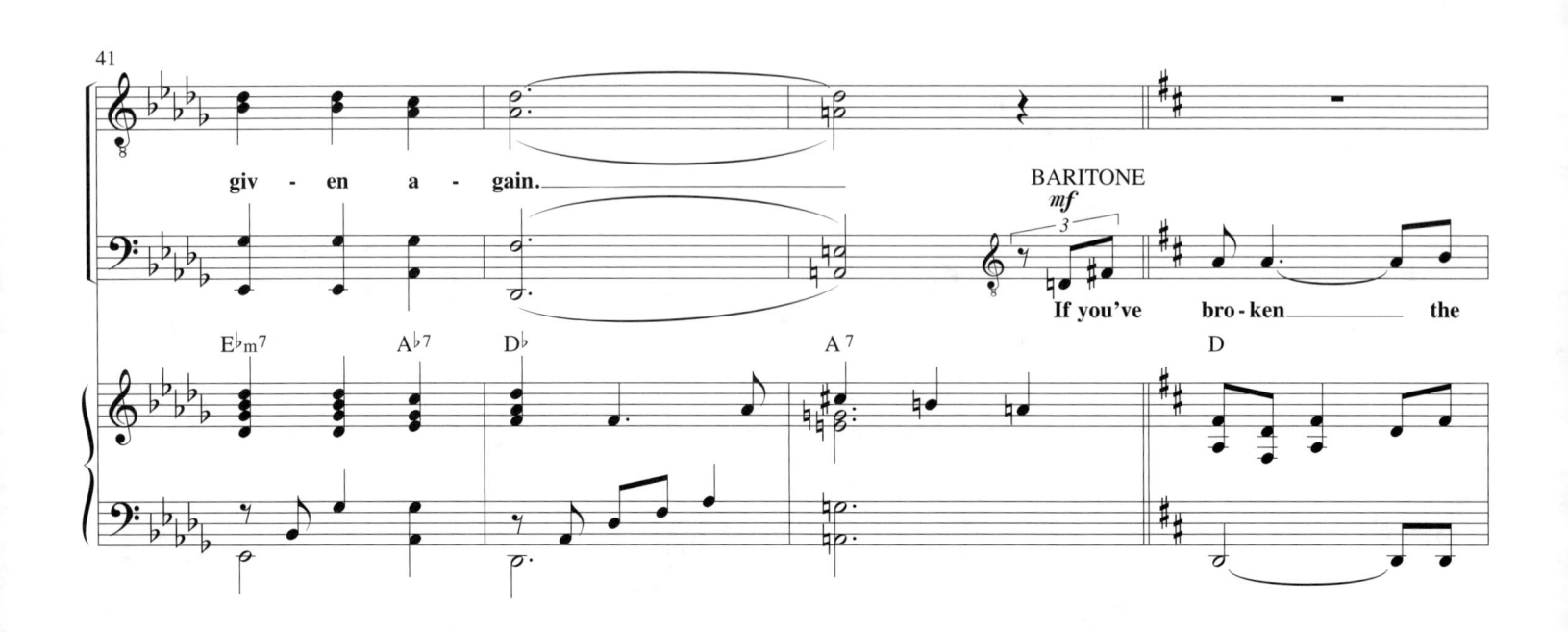

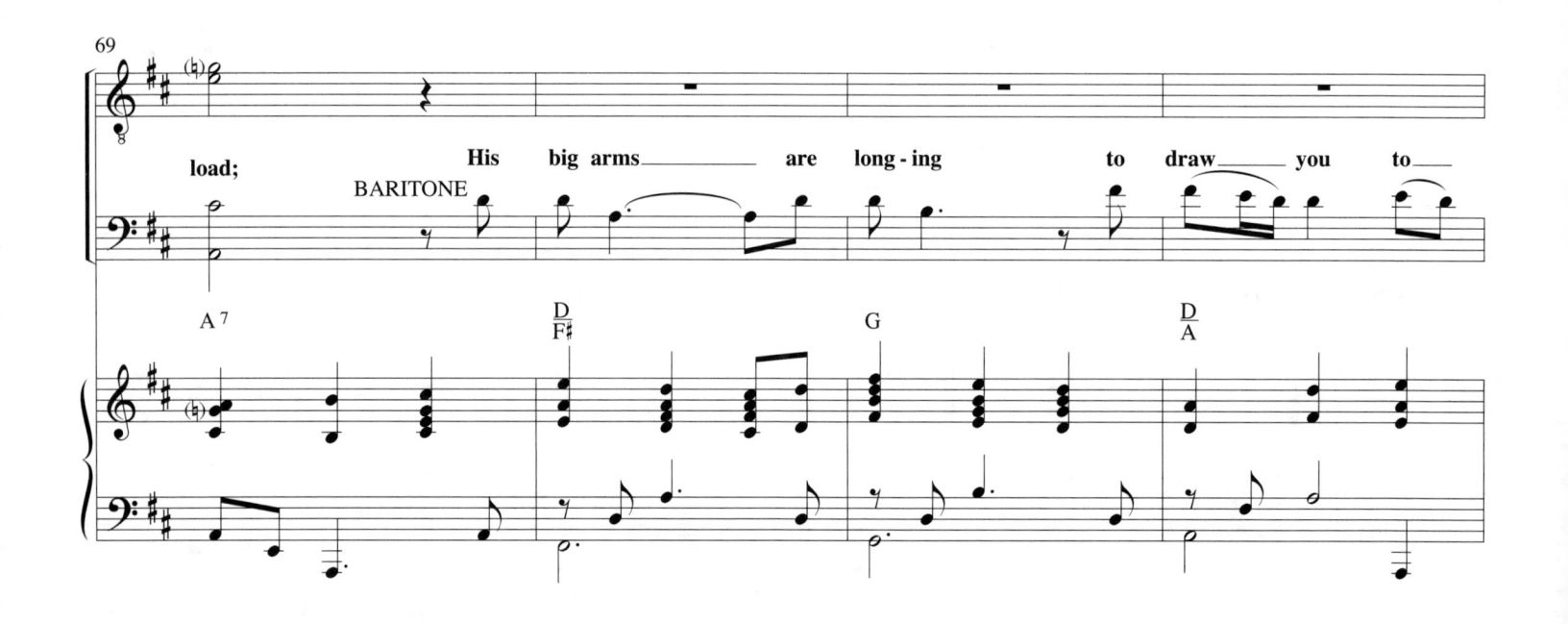

84

Reprise

Forgiven, _____ I'm forgiven,

forgiven, _____ I'm forgiven,

forgiven again. _____

He Made a Change

Originally from the album "Get Away, Jordan"

Words and Music by
ERNIE HAASE and JOEL LINDSEY

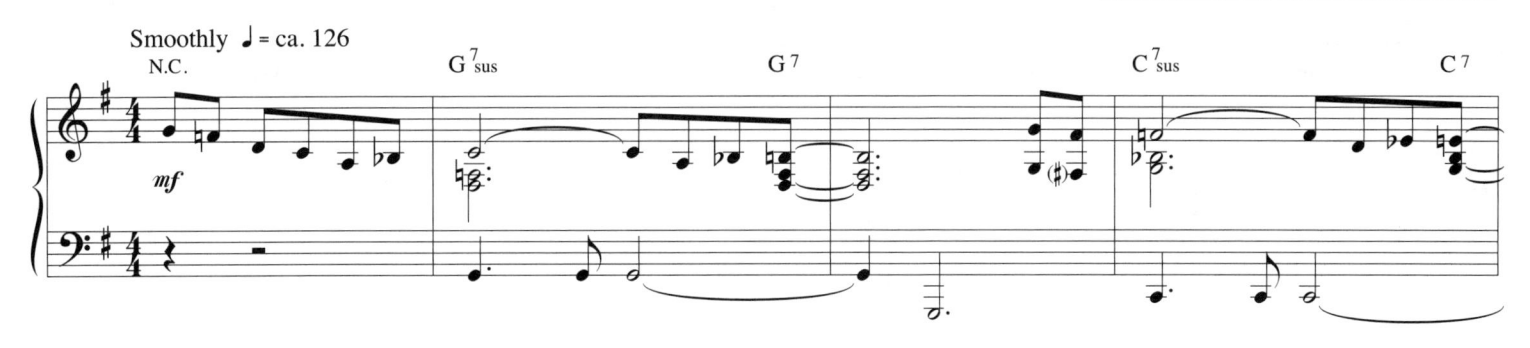

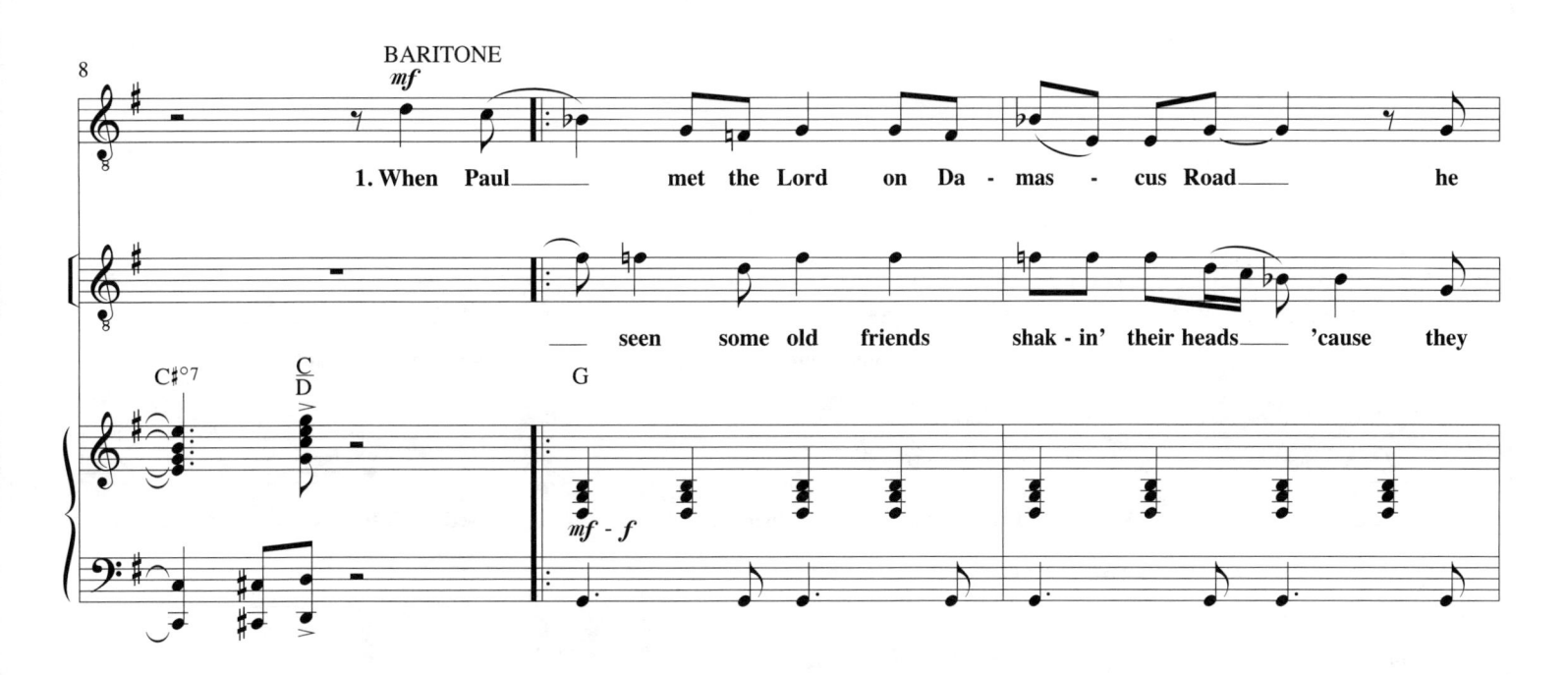

1. When Paul met the Lord on Da - mas - cus Road he

seen some old friends shak - in' their heads 'cause they

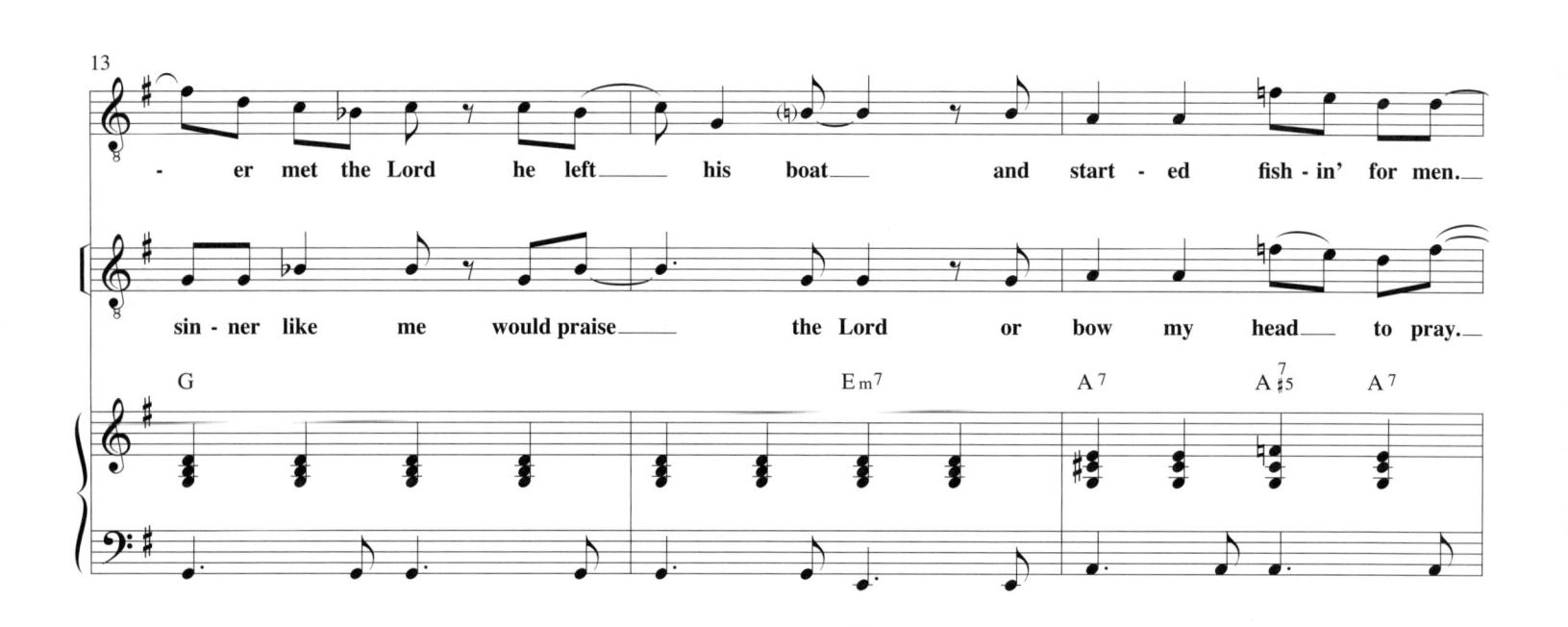

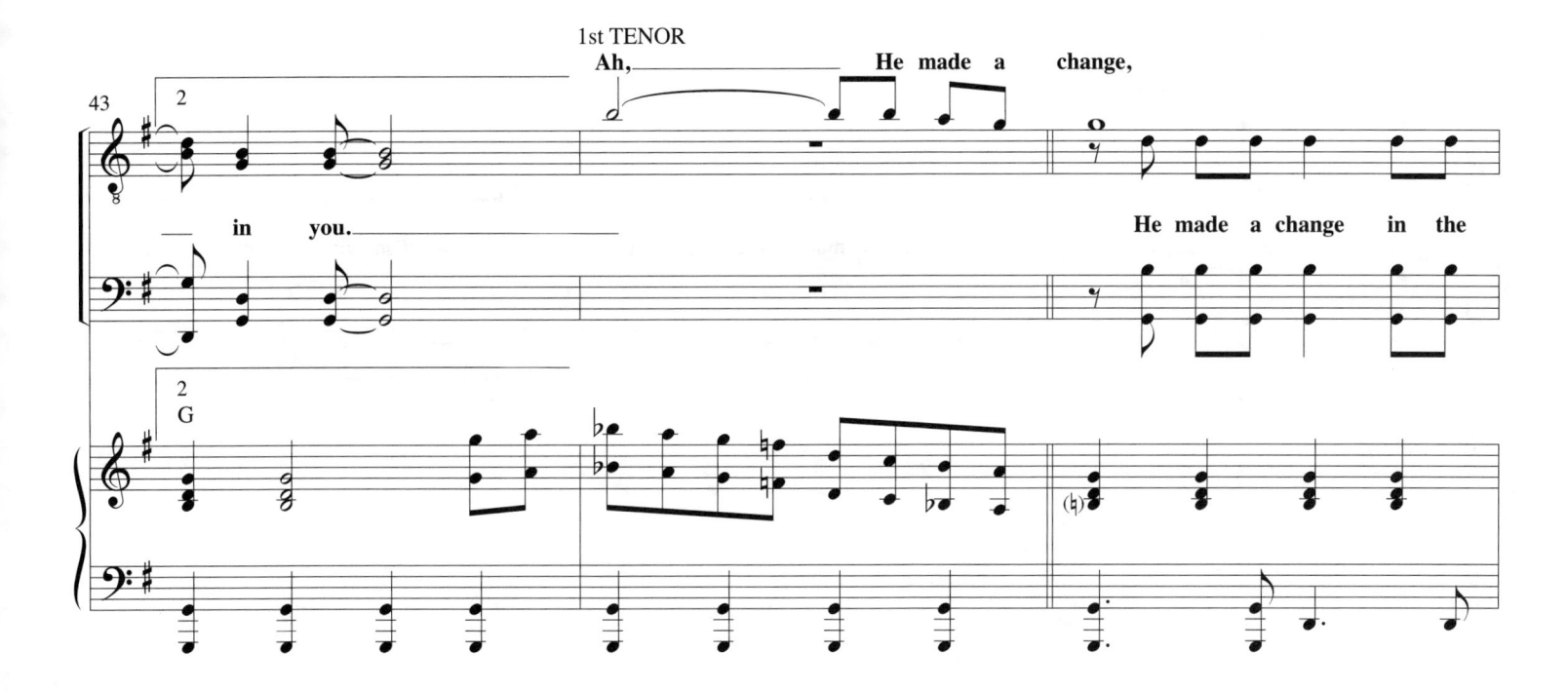

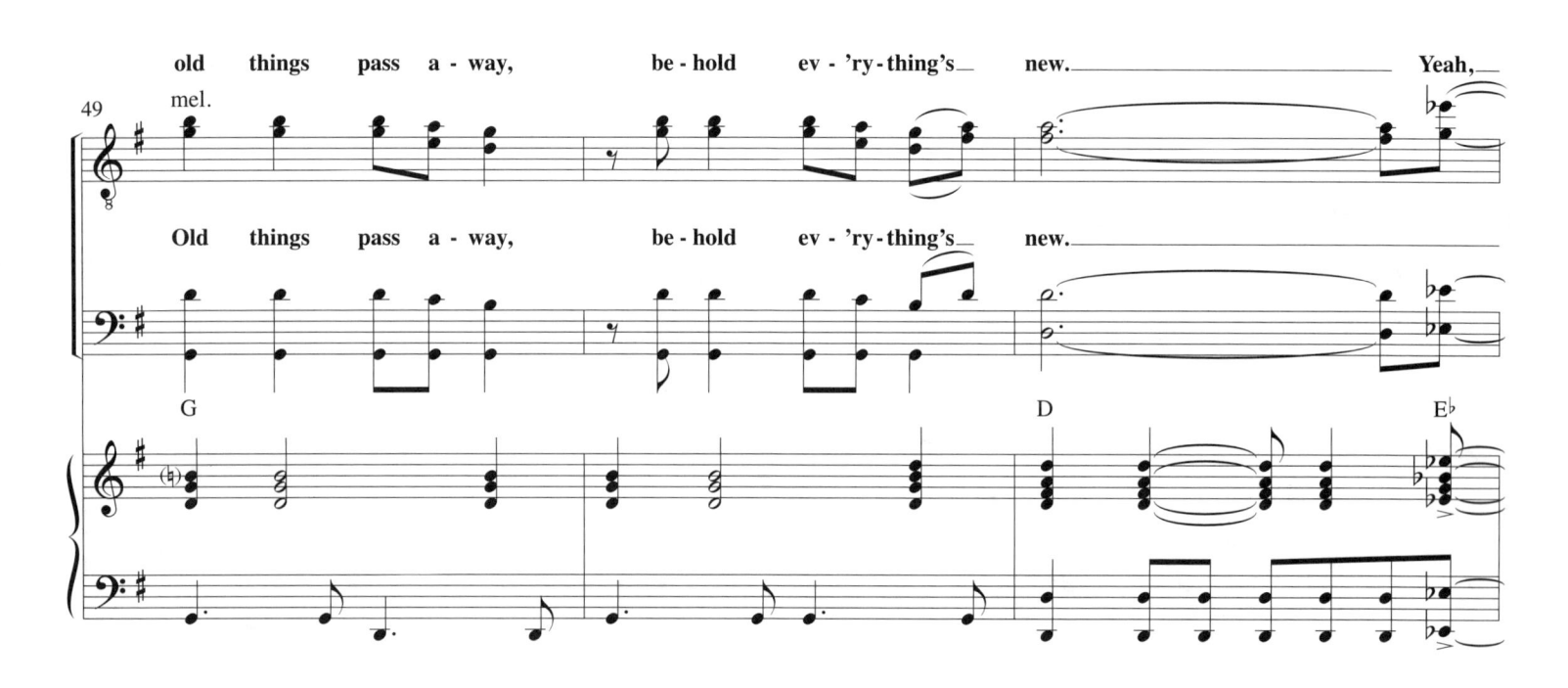

born a-gain, set free, fi-nal-ly for-giv-en. He can make a change in me, He

can make a change in you.

BARITONE _I know if_

He can make a change in me, He_ can make a change_ in you._

I Then Shall Live

Originally from the album "Together - Gaither Vocal Band and Ernie Haase & Signature Sound"

GLORIA GAITHER

JEAN SIBELIUS

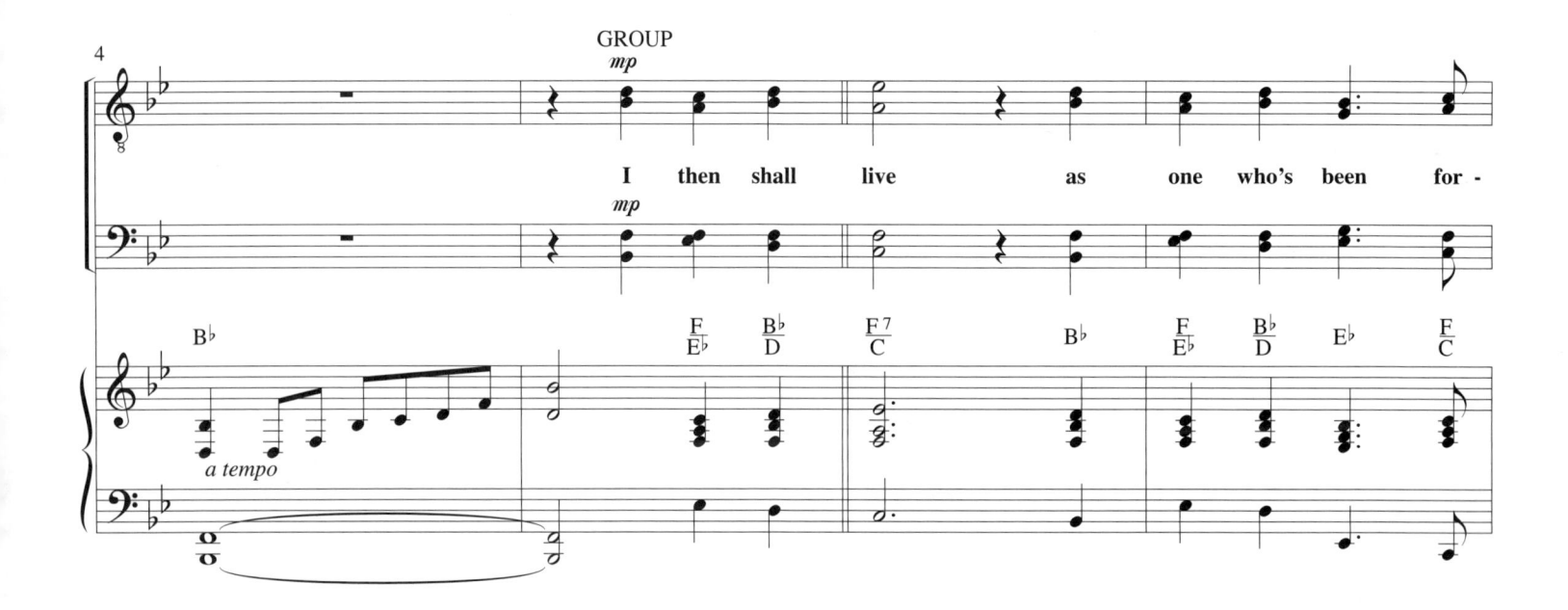

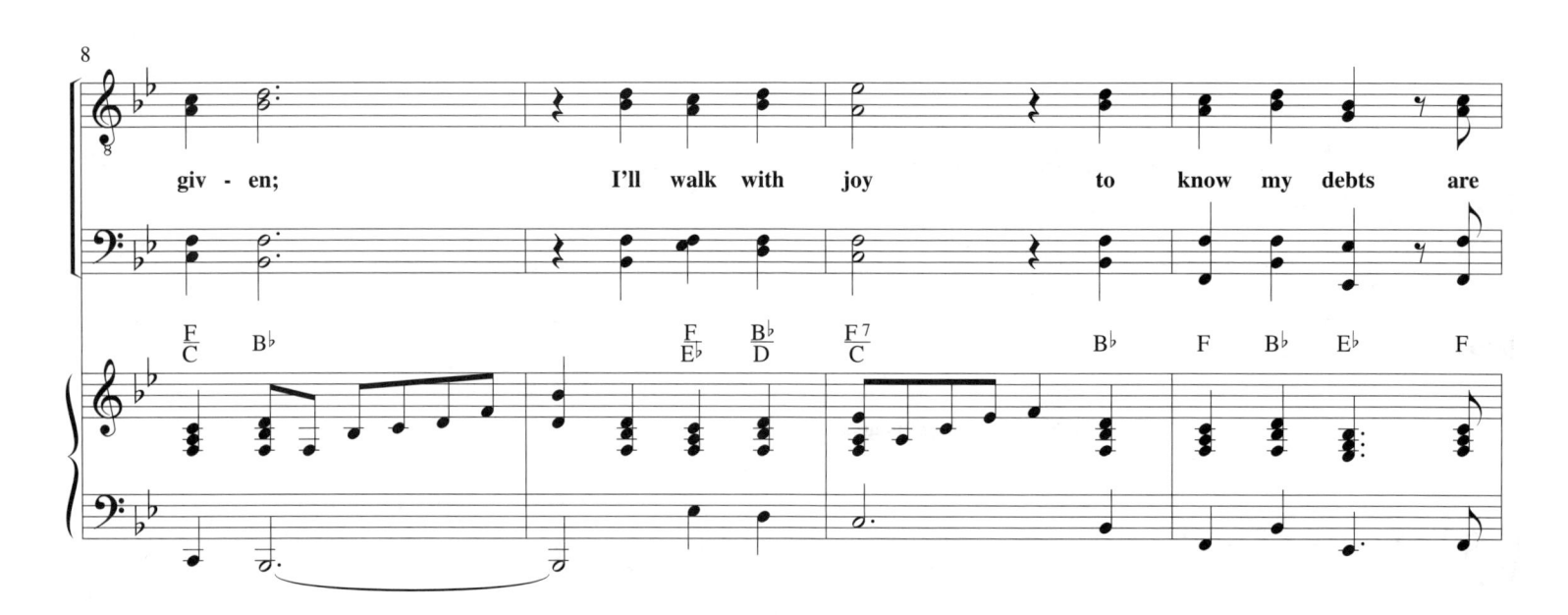

paid. I know my name is clear be - fore my

Fa - ther; I am His child and I am not a -

fraid. So great - ly par - doned, I'll for - give

my broth-er; The law of love I

glad-ly will___ o-bey.

I then shall live as one who's learned com-

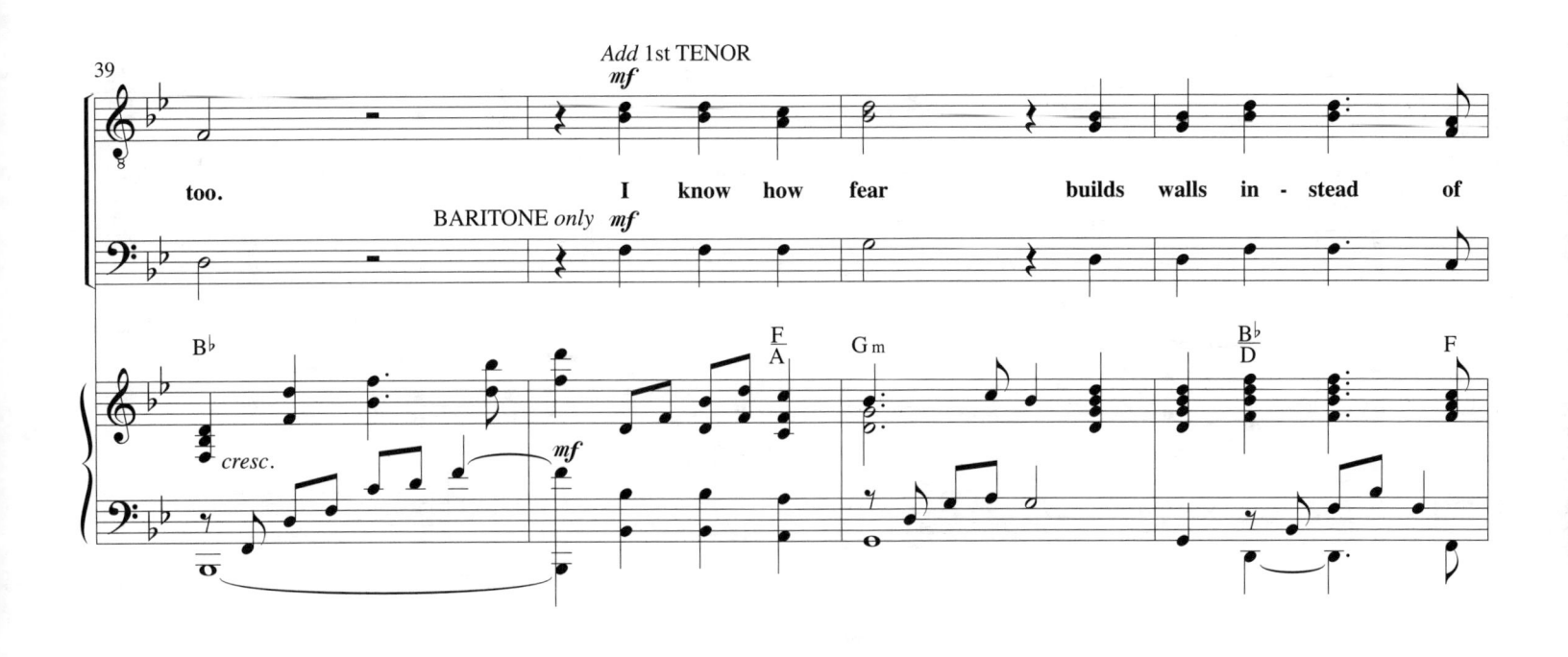

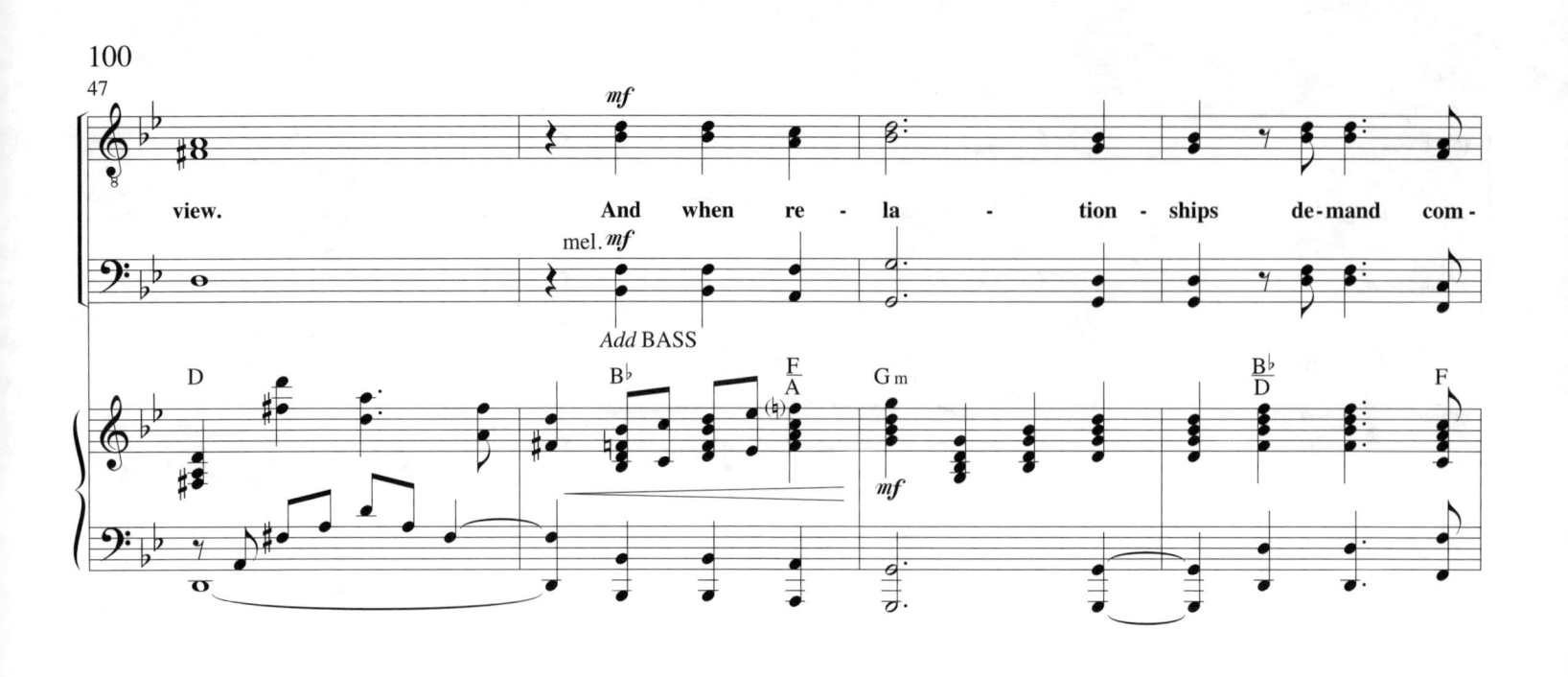

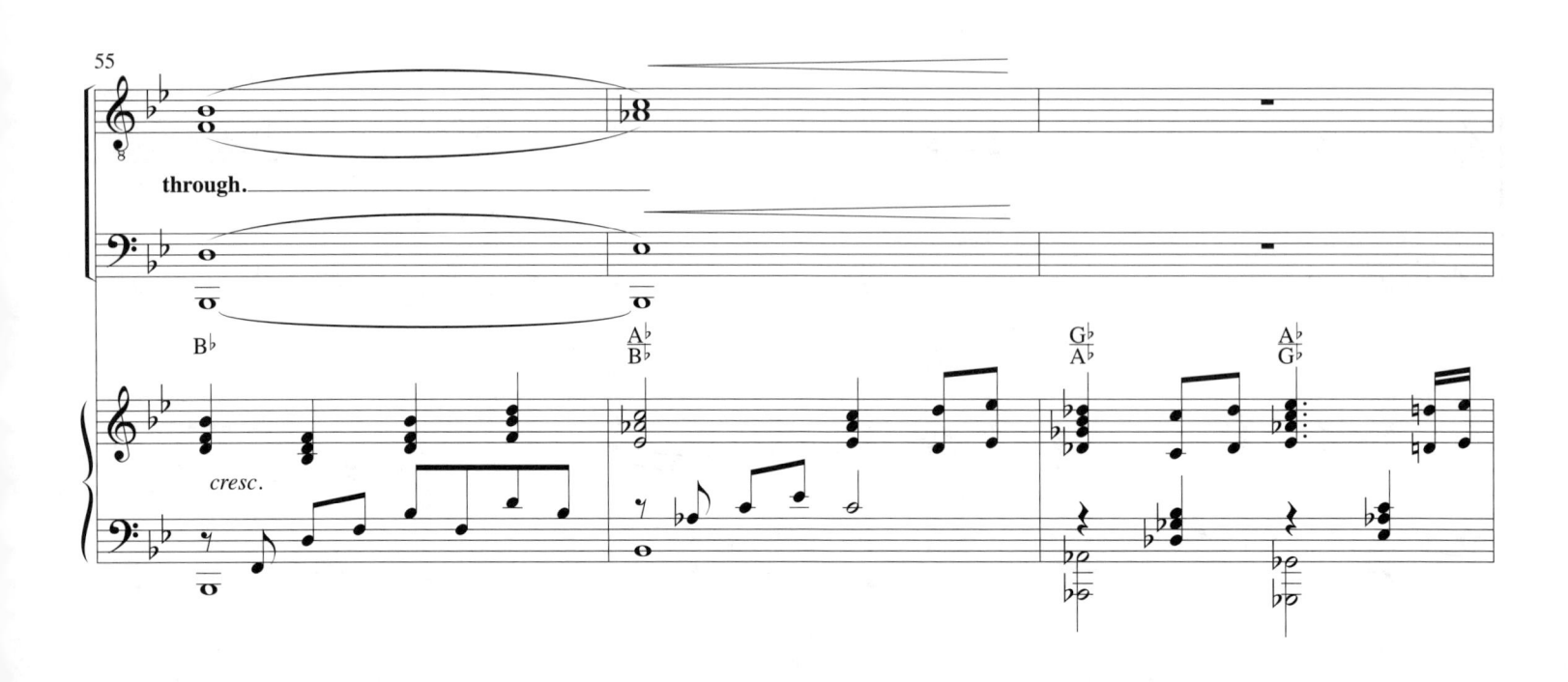

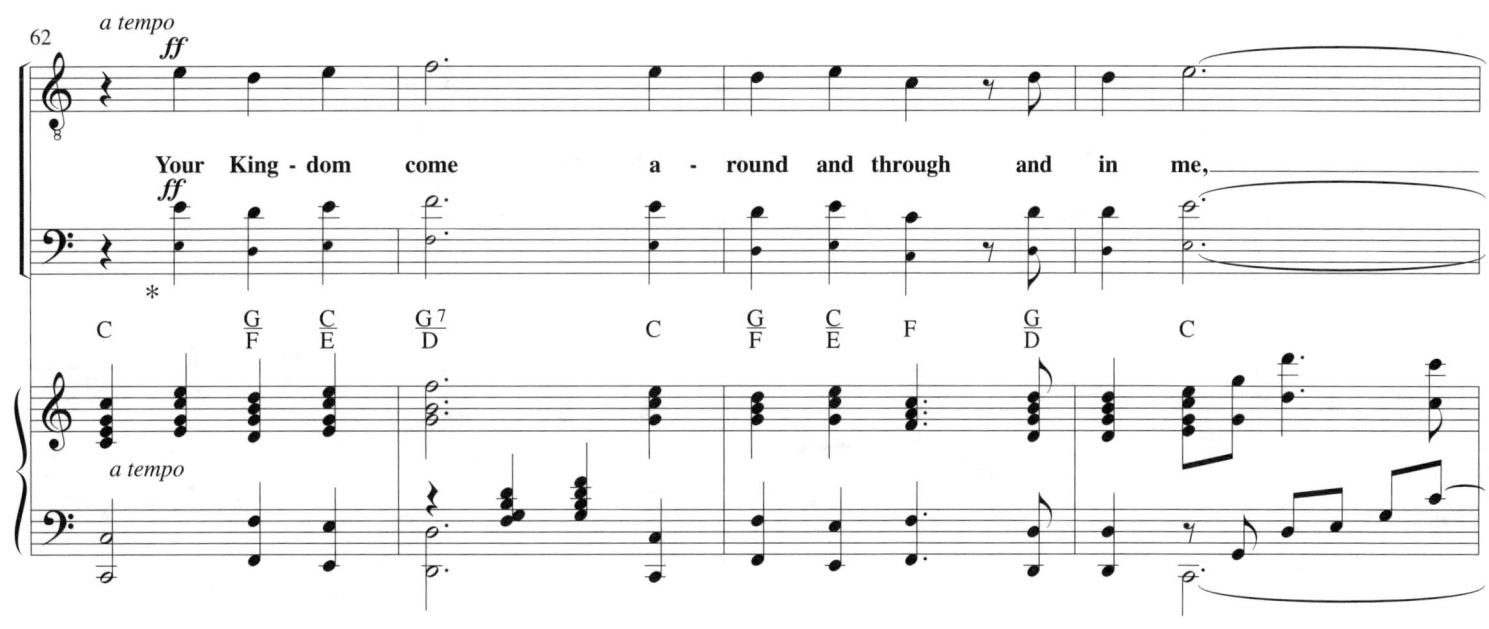

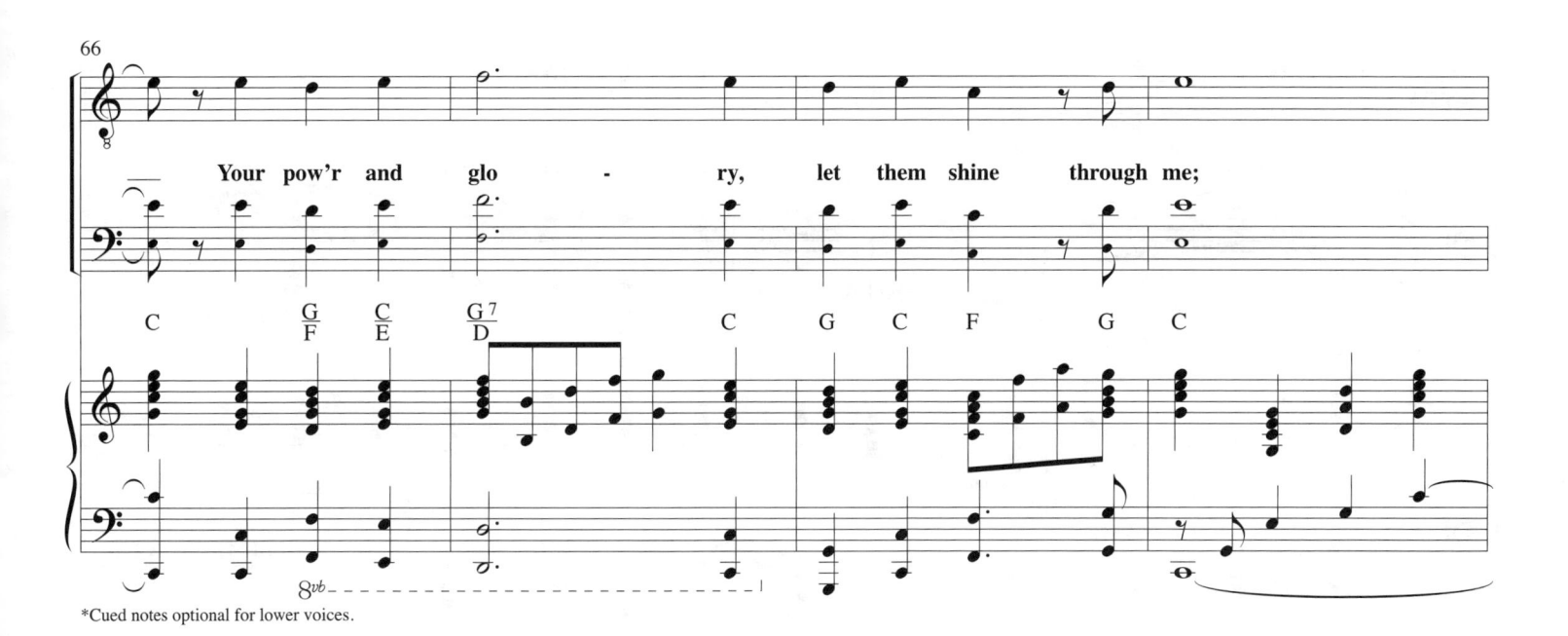

*Cued notes optional for lower voices.

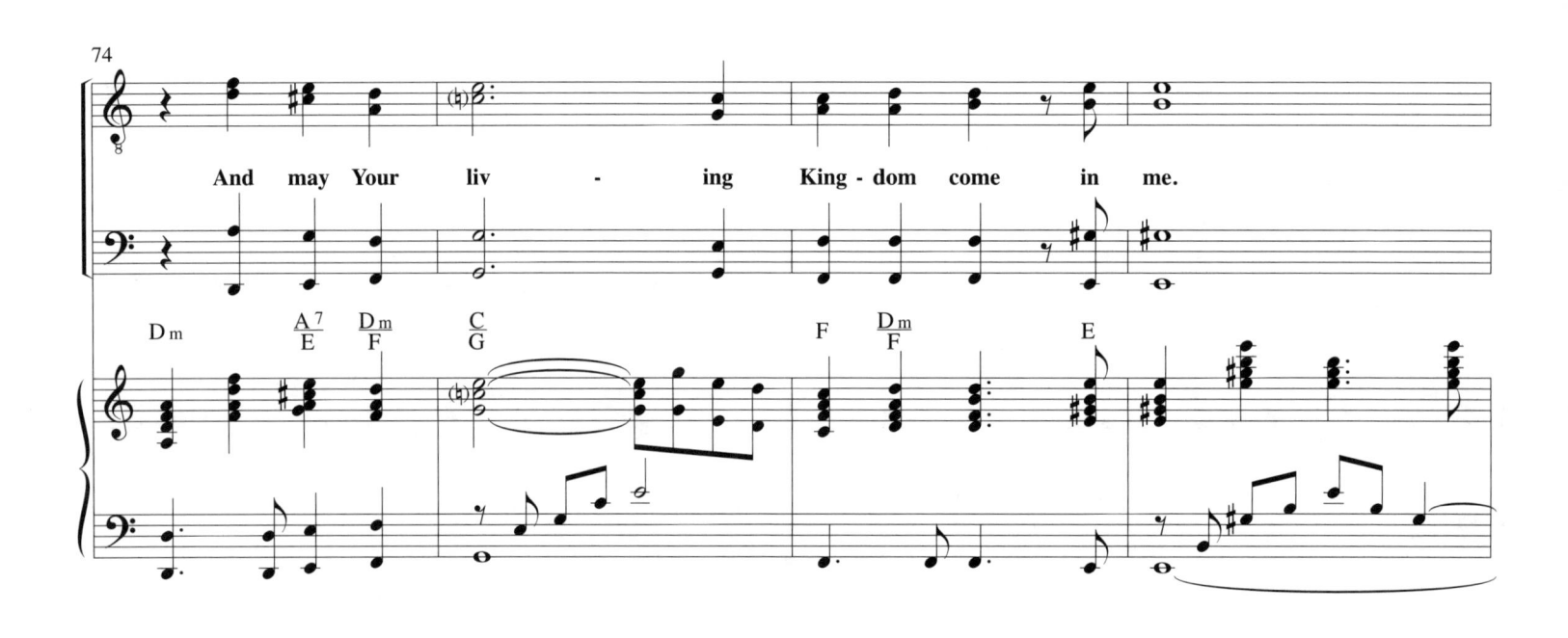

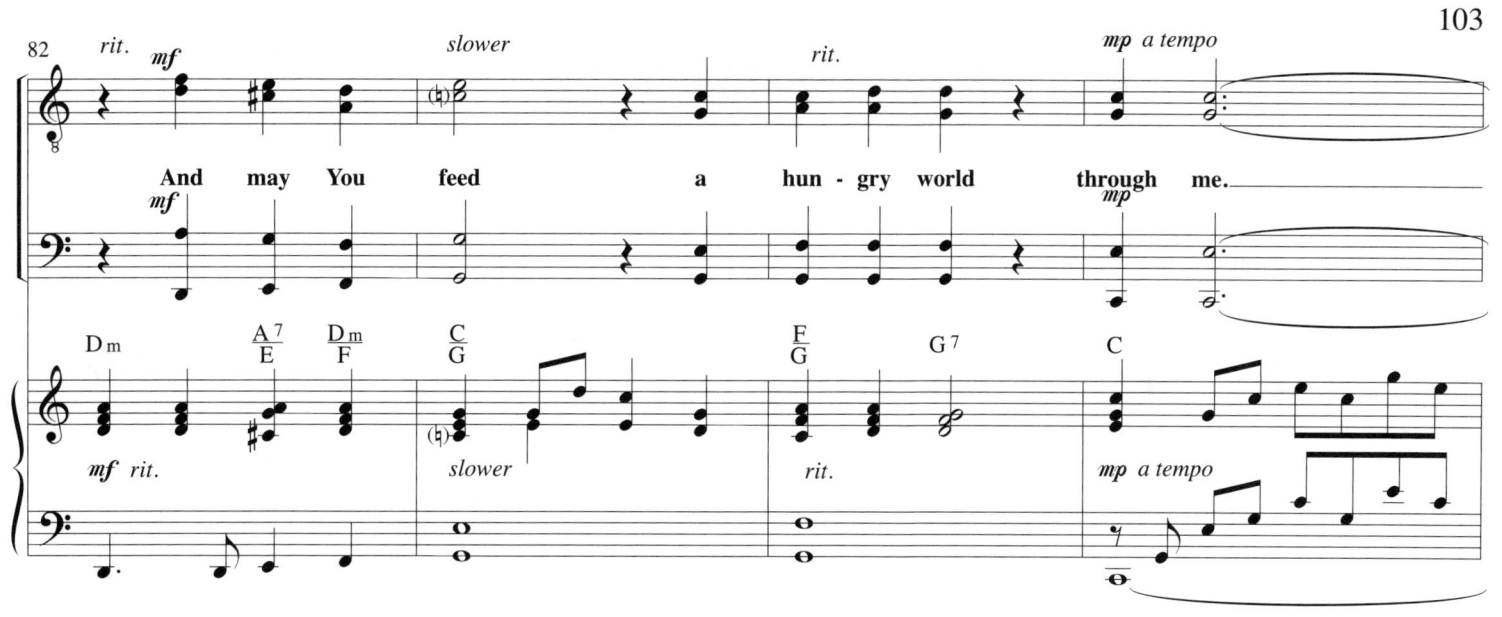

And may You feed a hun-gry world through me.

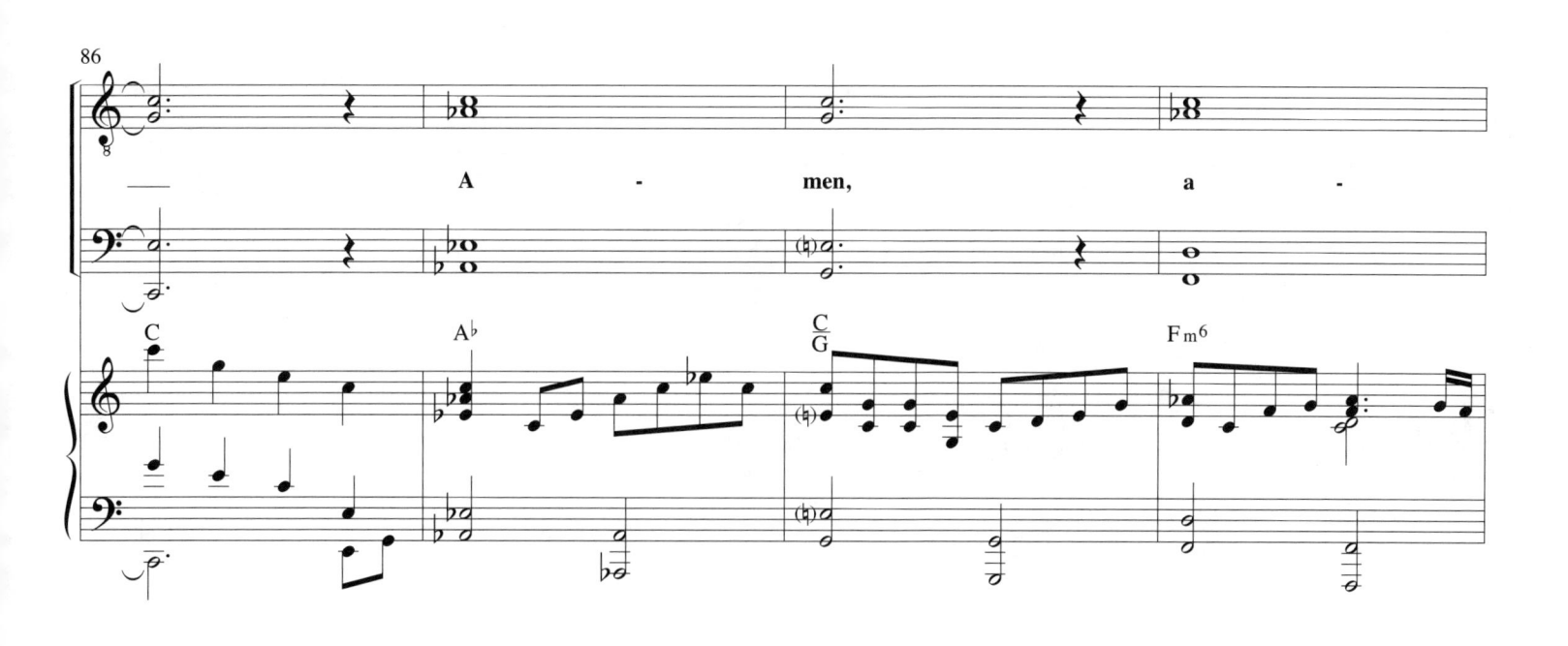

A - men, a -

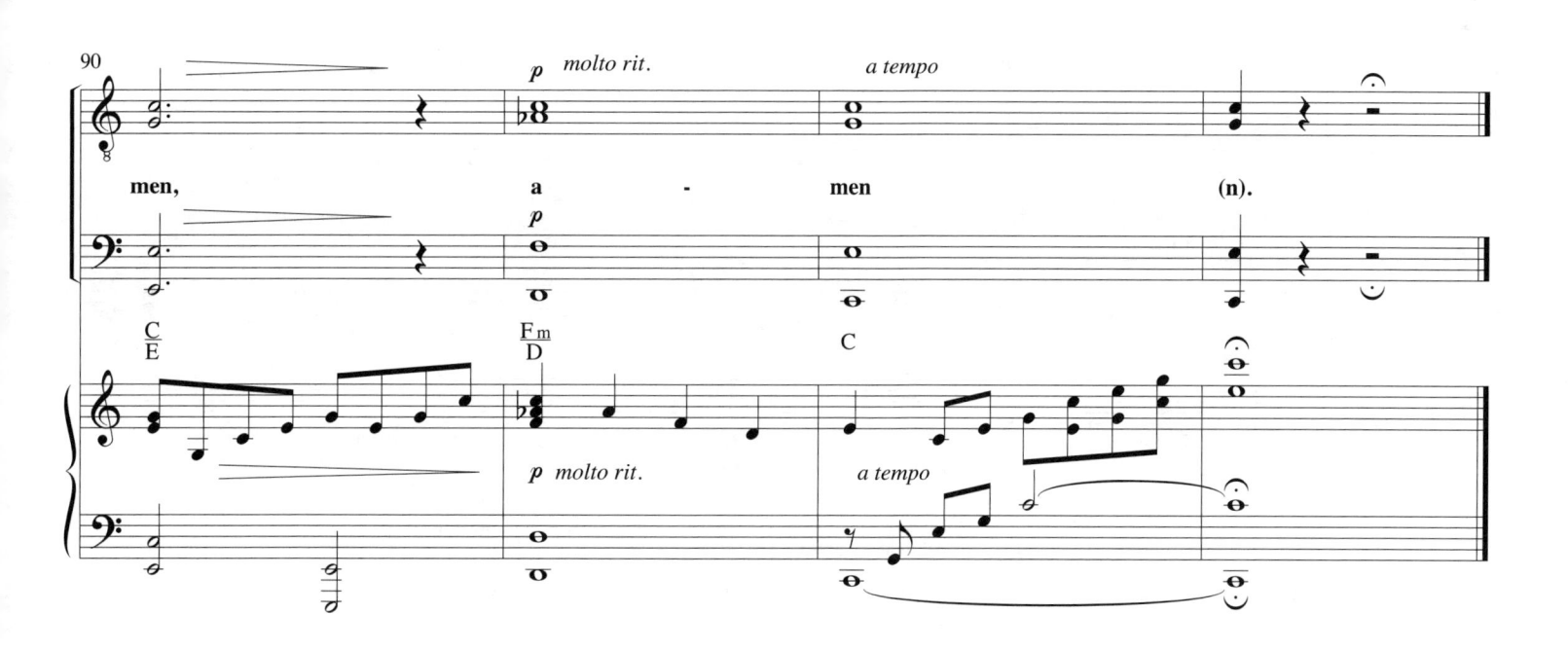

men, a - men (n).

Glory to God in the Highest

Originally from the album "Christmas with Ernie Haase & Signature Sound"

Words and Music by
DARYL WILLIAMS

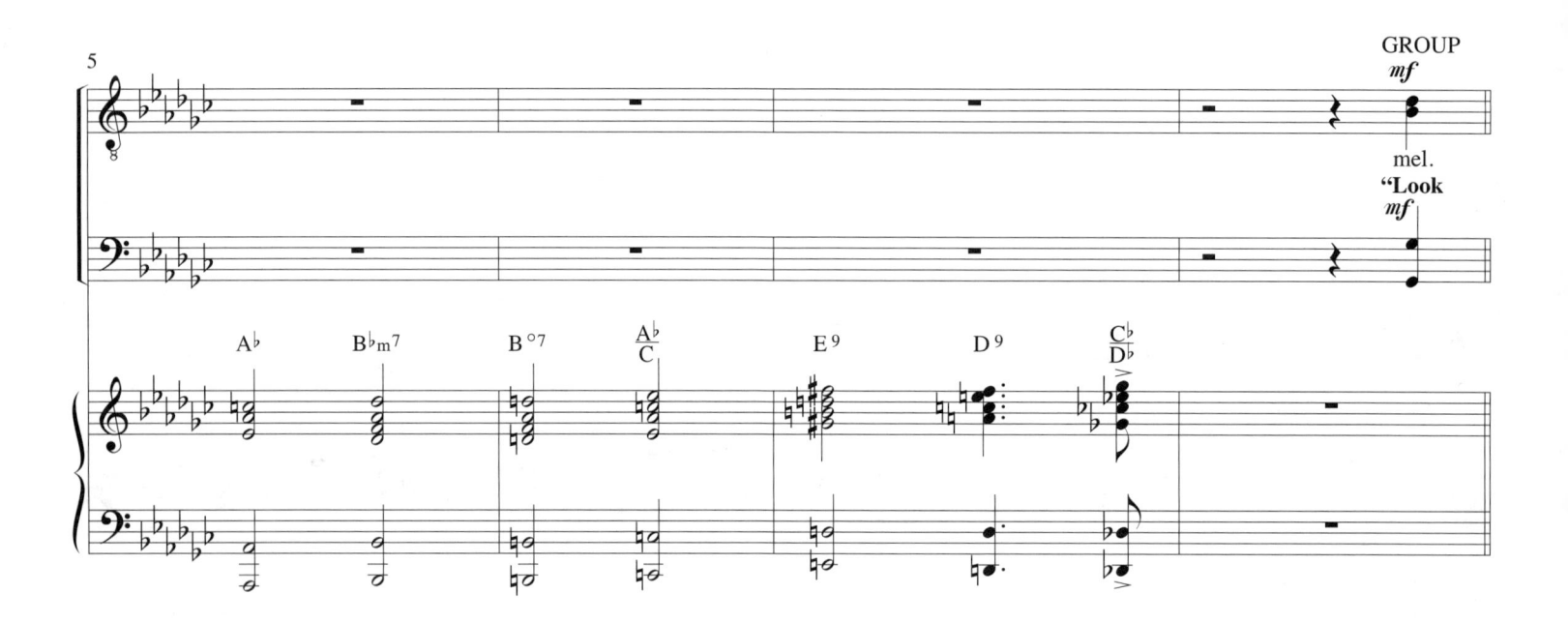

PLEASE NOTE: Copying of this product is NOT covered by CCLI licenses. For CCLI information call 1-800-234-2446.

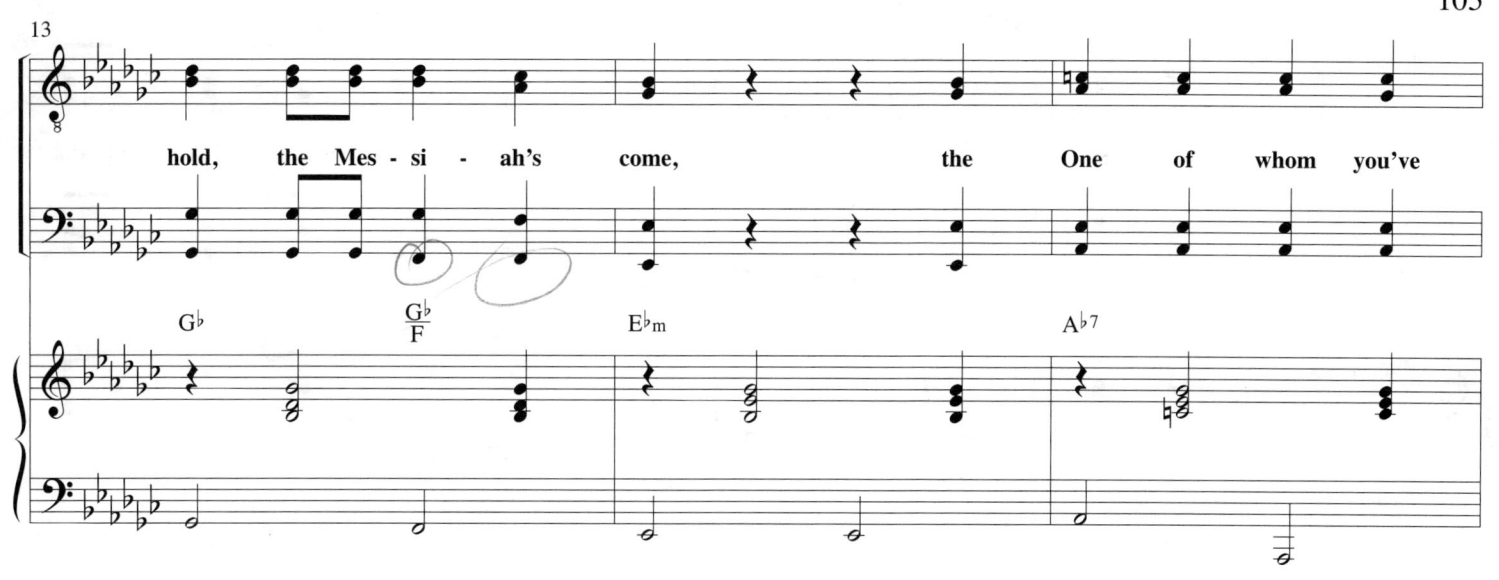

hold, the Mes - si - ah's come, the One of whom you've

G♭   G♭/F   E♭m   A♭7

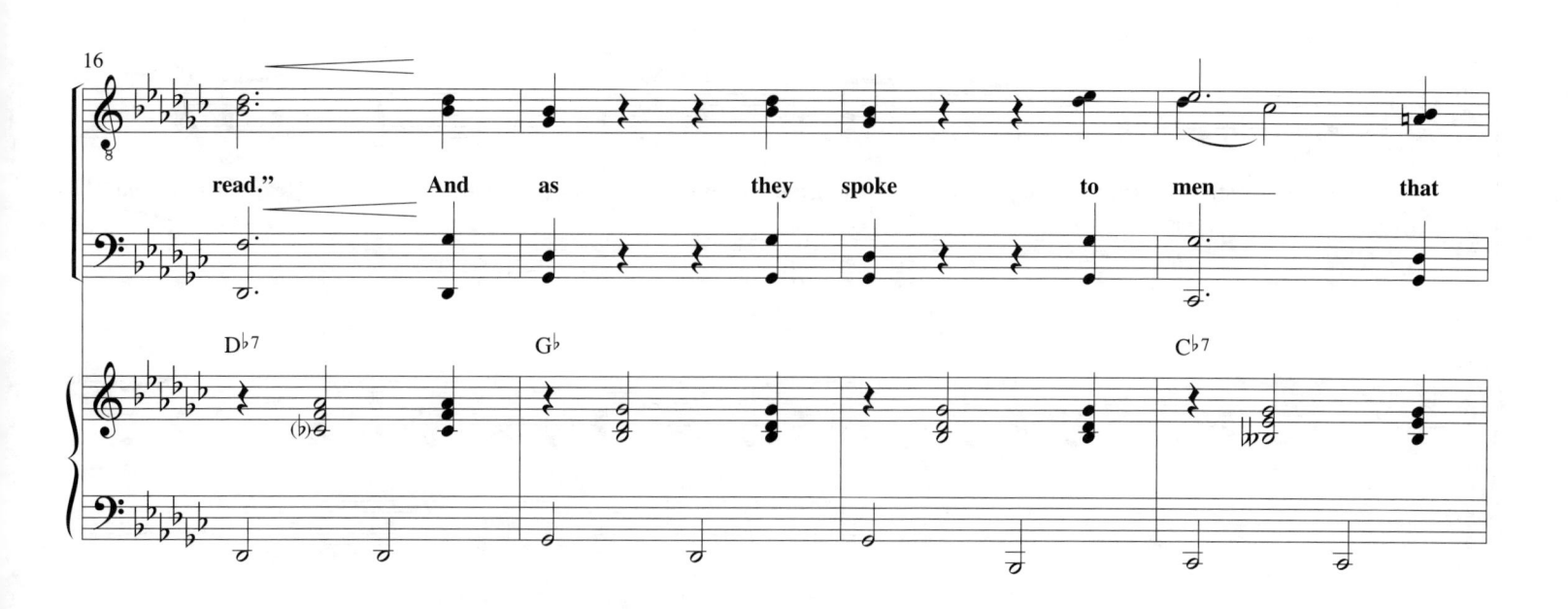

read." And as they spoke to men_____ that

D♭7   G♭   C♭7

day, The heav - en - ly host a - round_____ the throne joined

G♭   G♭/F   E♭m

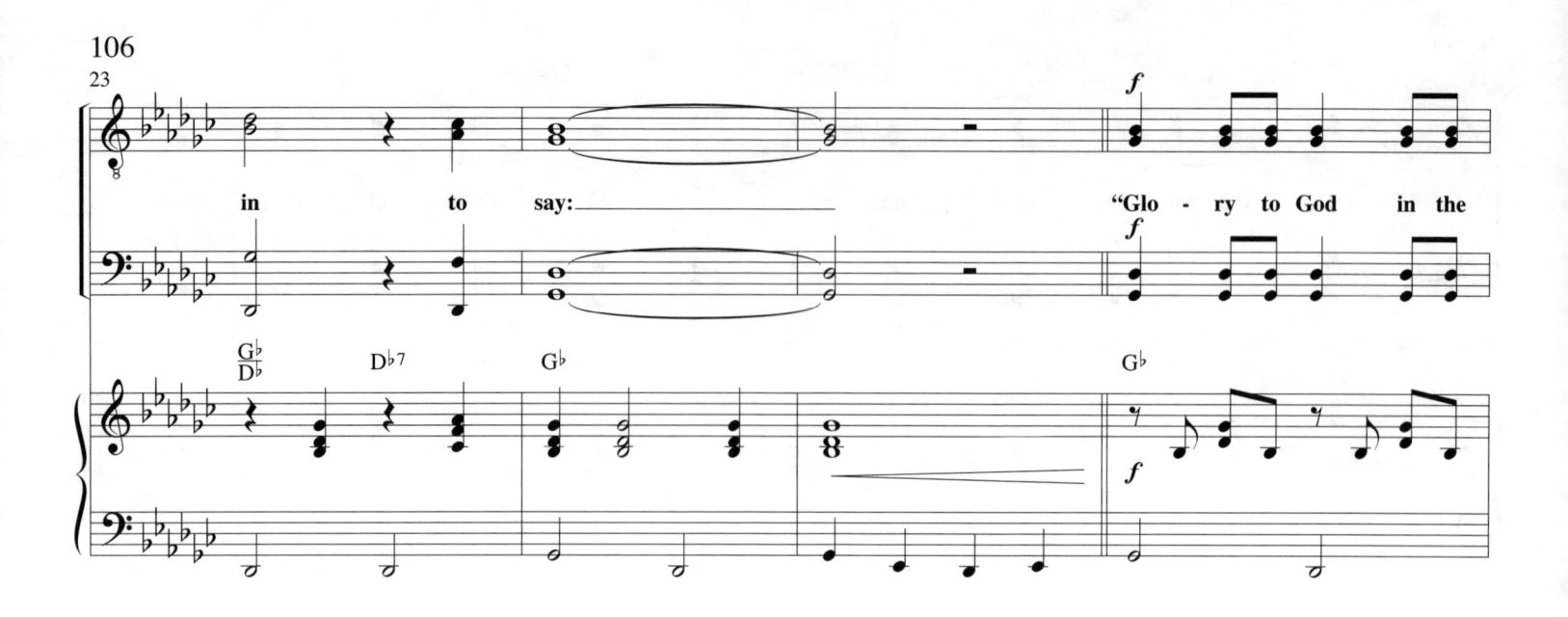

in to say:_____ "Glo - ry to God in the

high - est, peace on earth___ and good - will to men." Heav-en - ly an -

- gels an-nounced His ar - ri - val in the lit - tle town of Beth - le -

hem. Hal - le - lu - jah to the Lord sing ho - ly; He was born___ to save the world from

sin. Glo - ry to God in the high - est, glo - ry, hal - le - lu - jah to the Lord, a -

men._____

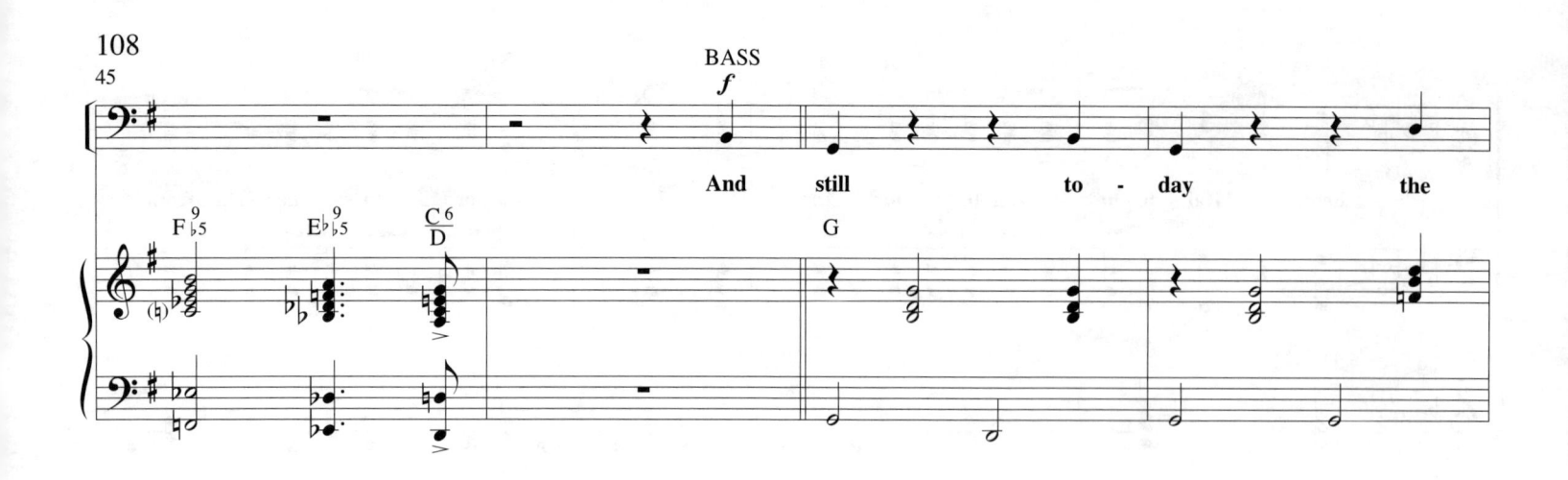

And still to - day the

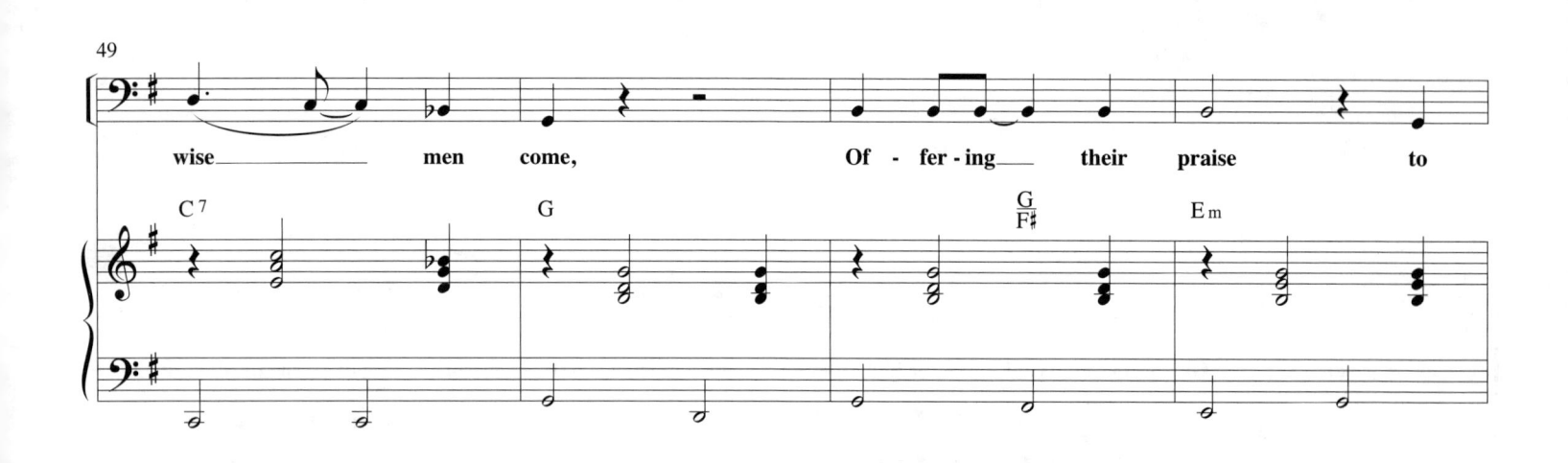

wise____ men come, Of - fer - ing____ their praise to

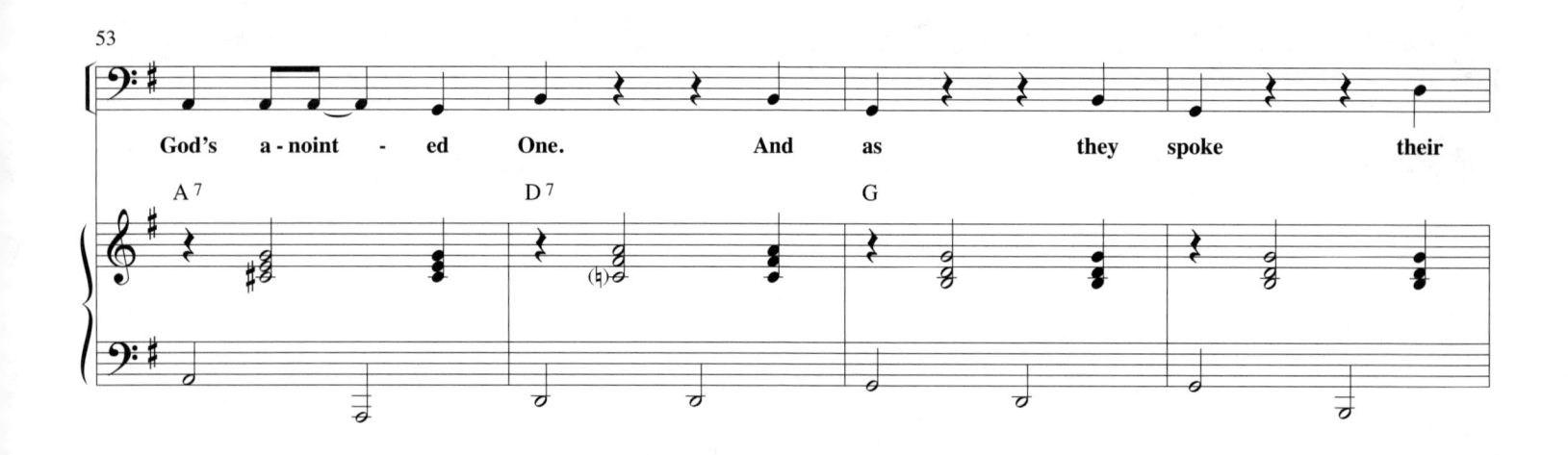

God's a - noint - ed One. And as they spoke their

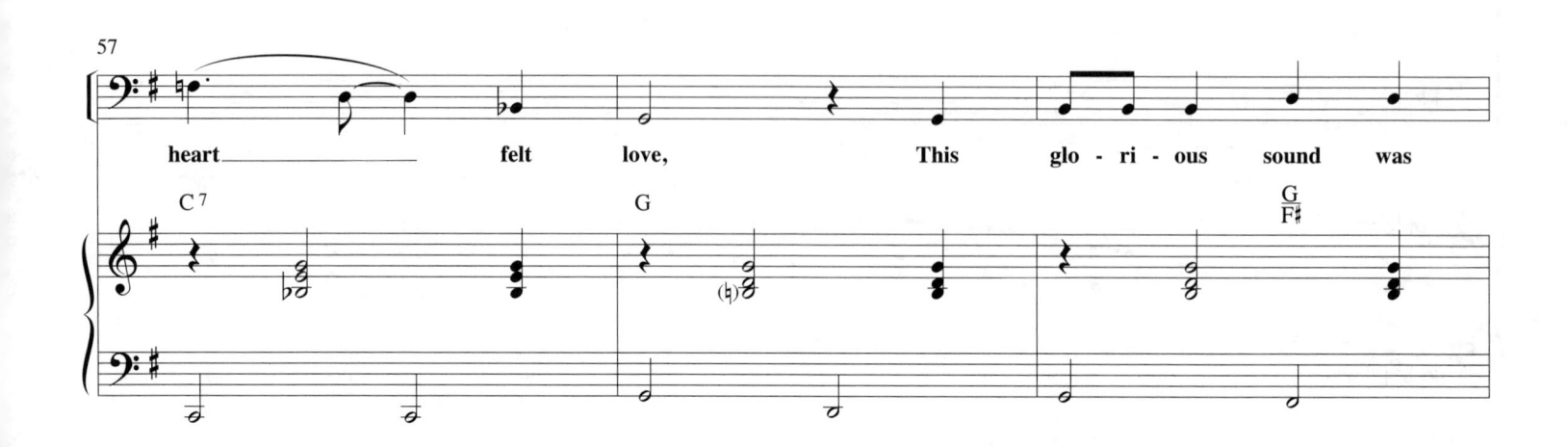

heart____ felt love, This glo - ri - ous sound was

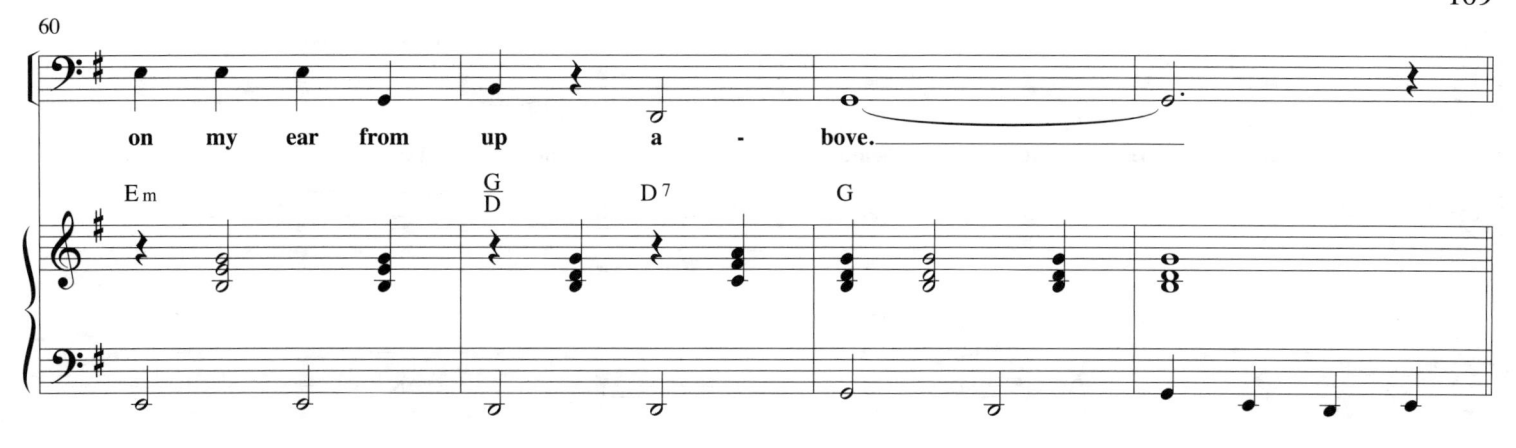

on my ear from up a - bove.

GROUP

"Glo - ry to God in the high - est, peace on earth and good - will to

men." Heav-en - ly an - gels an-nounced His ar - ri - val in the lit - tle

town of Beth - le - hem. Hal - le - lu - jah to the Lord sing

ho - ly; He was born___ to save the world from sin. Glo - ry to

God in the high - est, glo - ry, hal - le - lu - jah to the Lord, a - men.

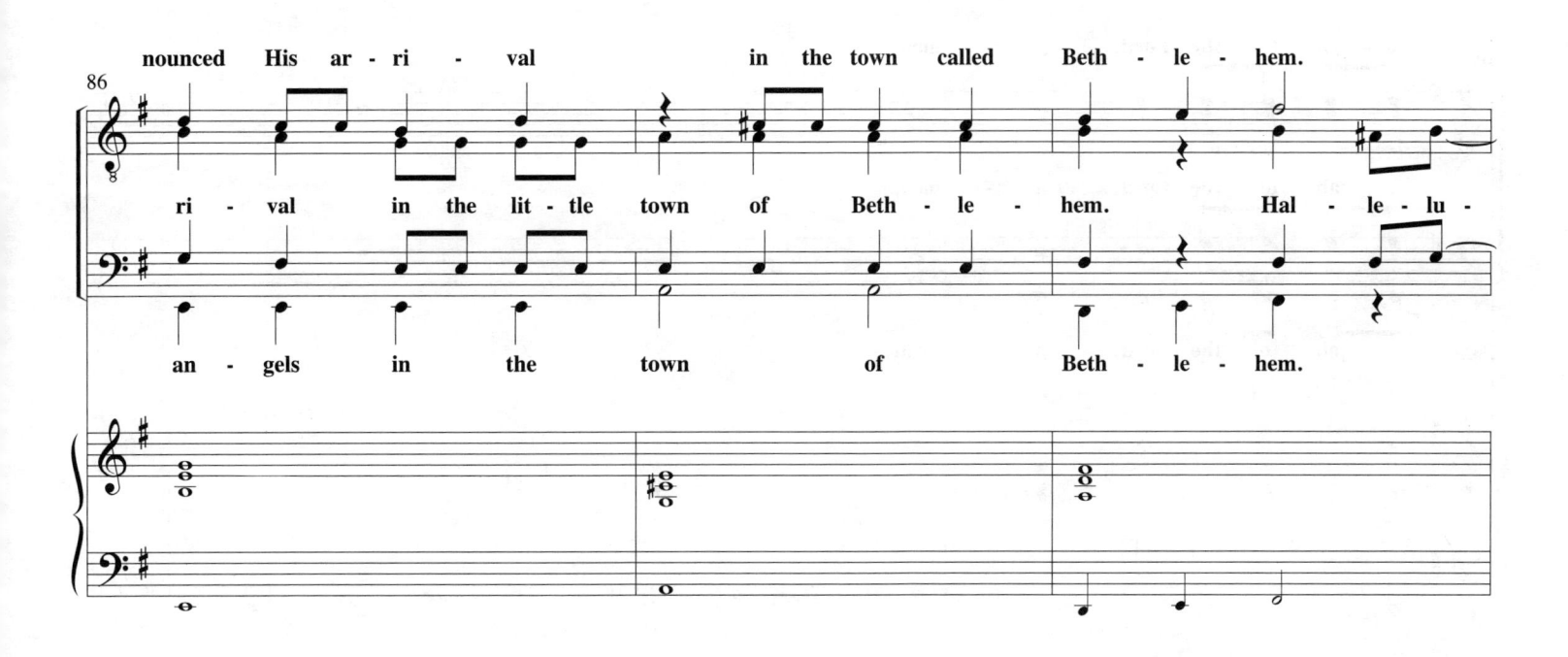

"Glo - ry to God in the high - est, peace on earth___ and good - will to

men." Heav-en - ly an - gels an-nounced His ar - ri - val in the lit - tle

town of Beth - le - hem. Hal - le - lu - jah to the Lord sing

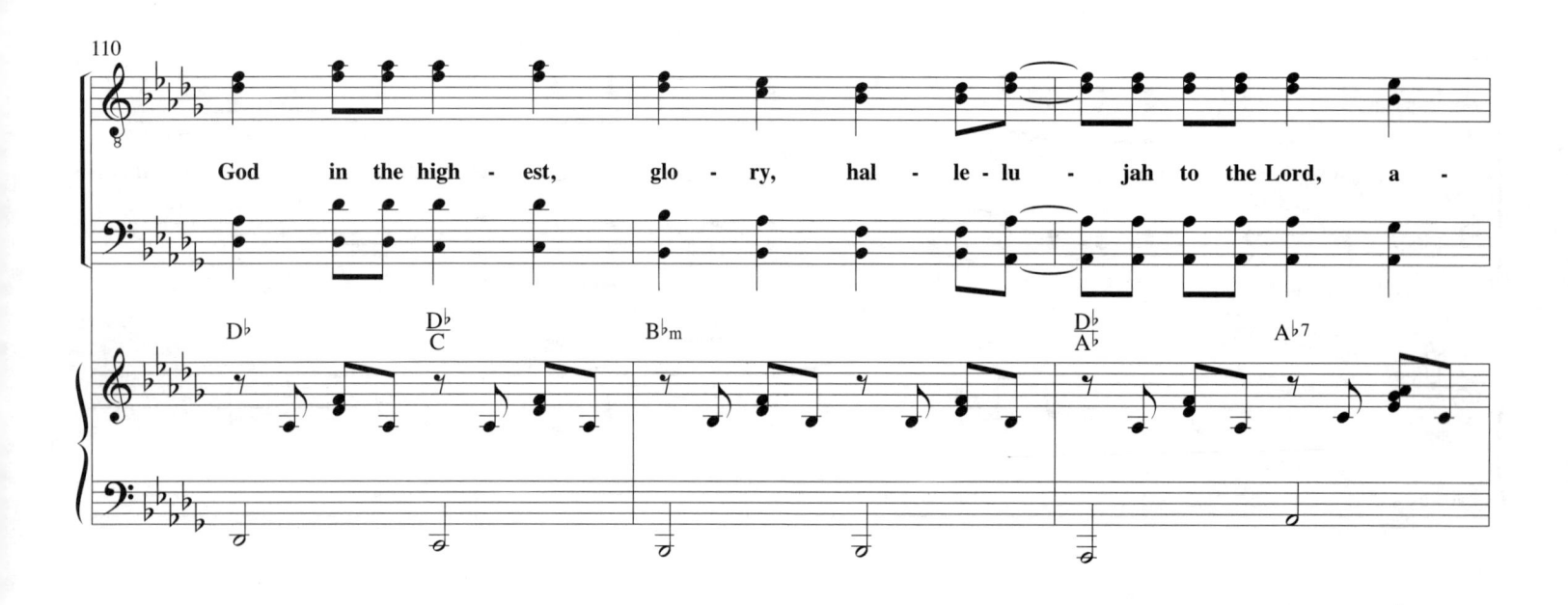

Heav-en-ly an - gels an-nounced His ar -
and good - will to men."

ri - val in the lit - tle town of Beth - le - hem. Hal - le - lu -

jah to the Lord sing ho - ly; He was born to save the world from

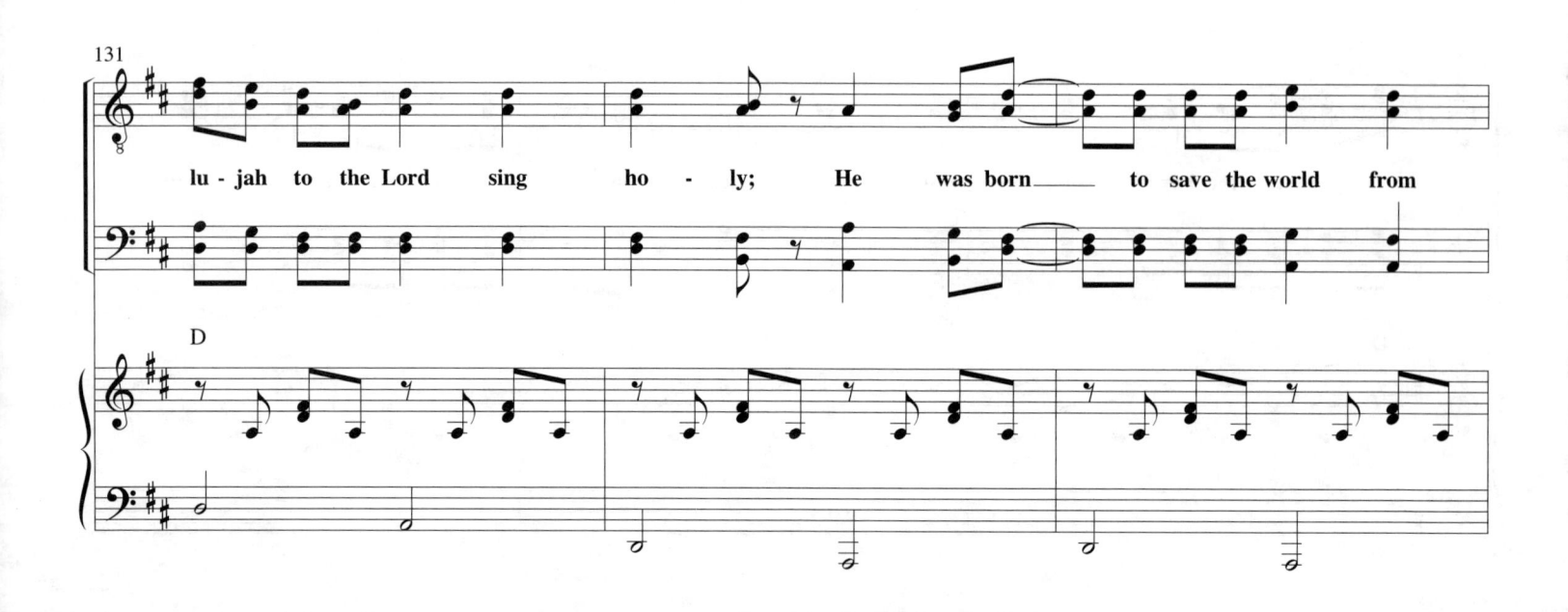

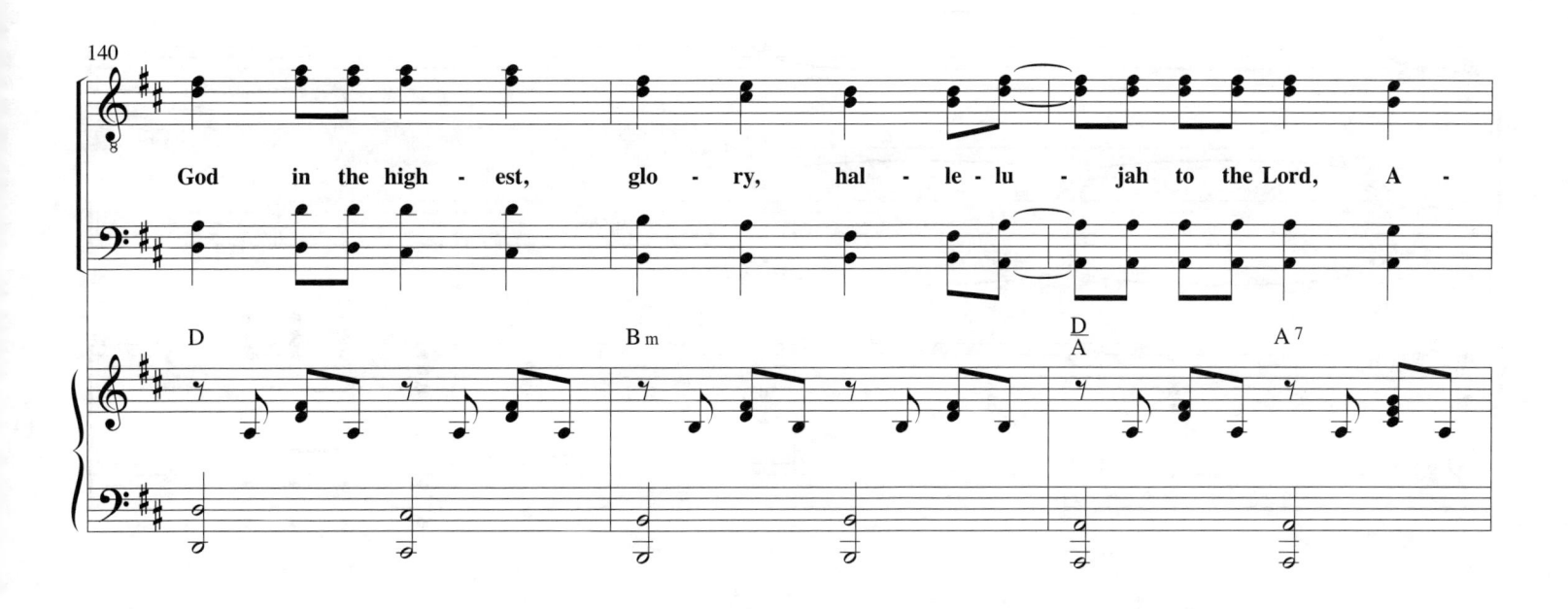

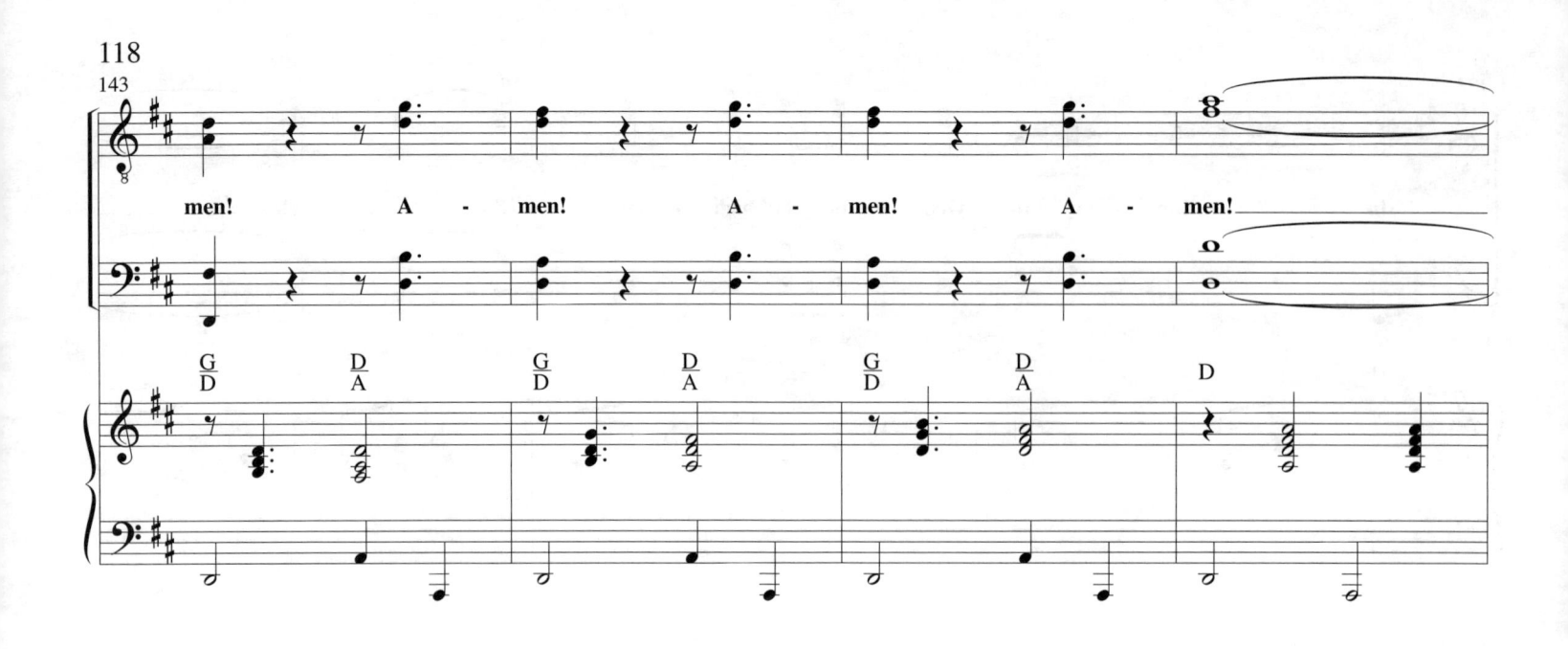

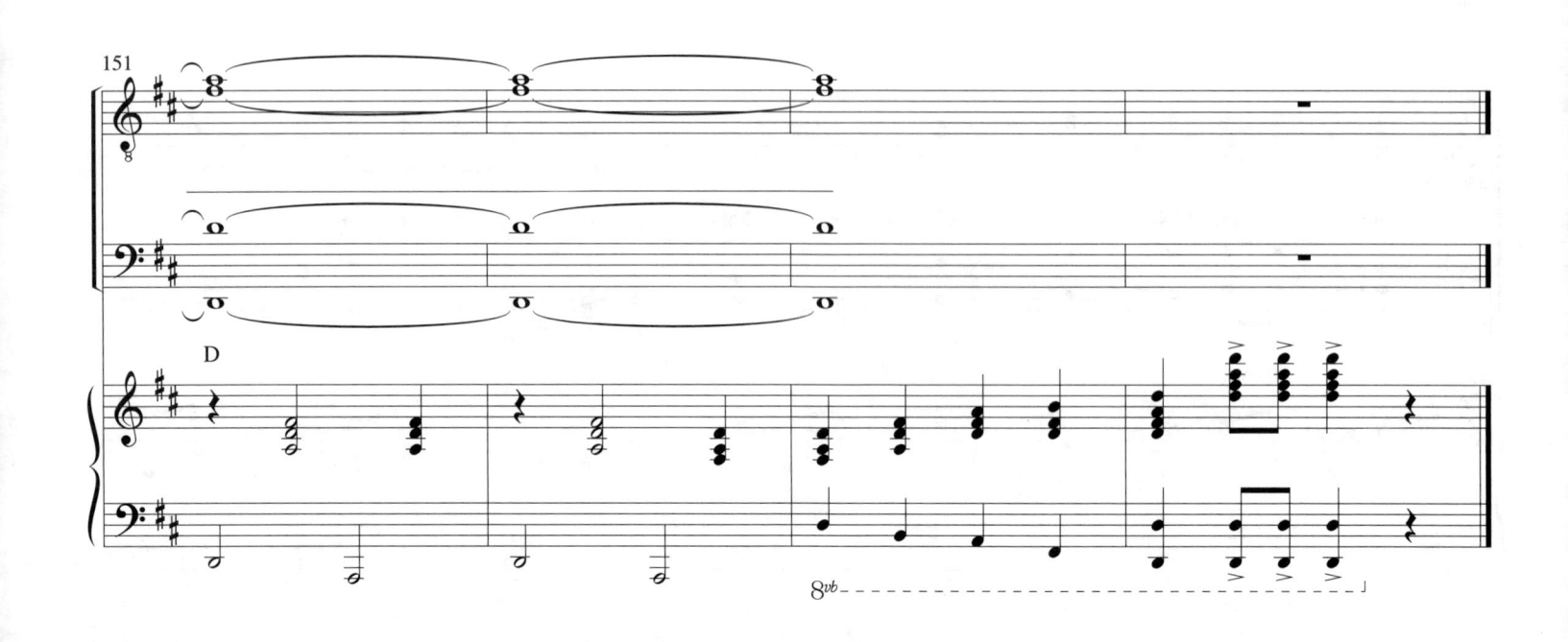